WELCOMING YOUR PUPPY
FROM PLANET DOG

Also by Kathy Callahan

101 Rescue Puppies:
One Family's Story of Fostering Dogs, Love, and Trust

WELCOMING YOUR PUPPY
FROM PLANET DOG

How to Go Beyond Training and Raise Your Best Friend

KATHY CALLAHAN, CPDT-KA

New World Library
Novato, California

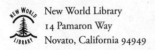

New World Library
14 Pamaron Way
Novato, California 94949

Text design by Tona Pearce Myers

Library of Congress Cataloging-in-Publication Data

Names: Callahan, Kathy, author.
Title: Welcoming your puppy from planet dog : how to go beyond training and raise your best friend / Kathy Callahan, CPDT-KA.
Description: Novato, California : New World Library, [2024] | Includes bibliographical references and index. | Summary: "An innovative, engaging guide that teaches dog owners how to train a puppy by working with, rather than against, the puppy's instincts. Includes advice on dealing with common issues such as house-breaking, chewing, jumping, and helping puppies live harmoniously with cats, other dogs, or children"--Provided by publisher.
Identifiers: LCCN 2023053737 (print) | LCCN 2023053738 (ebook) | ISBN 9781608689217 (paperback) | ISBN 9781608689224 (epub)
Subjects: LCSH: Puppies--Training. | Puppies--Behavior.
Classification: LCC SF431 .C34 2024 (print) | LCC SF431 (ebook) | DDC 636.7/0887--dc23/eng/20240102
LC record available at https://lccn.loc.gov/2023053737
LC ebook record available at https://lccn.loc.gov/2023053738

First printing, April 2024
ISBN 978-1-60868-921-7
Ebook ISBN 978-1-60868-922-4
Printed in Canada on 100% postconsumer-waste recycled paper

New World Library is proud to be a Gold Certified Environmentally Responsible Publisher. Publisher certification awarded by Green Press Initiative.

10   9   8   7   6   5   4   3   2   1

CONTENTS

Part 7: Being a Great Owner

INTRODUCTION

You Kidnapped Your Puppy from Another Planet

"What if this was a mistake?"

This secret thought — unutterable even to family members — keeps more than a few new puppy owners up at night. They tell me, sometimes in a whisper, that they must be missing something. Getting a puppy was supposed to be fun, but all they feel is stress, frustration — even anger.

They seek me out for the Magic Answers, the training tips that will bring peace. They are at their wit's end with the biting, the peeing, and the destruction. They get out their notebooks, ready to record expert information personalized for their situation.

I absolutely have those tips and tricks, strategies and game plans. Here's the problem: they're not going to work without the right mindset. There is actually just one thing I want new owners to write down in that notebook, so they can make it a part of every interaction they have with their puppy:

This is a baby that I kidnapped from another planet.

The way to enjoy puppyhood — and emerge from it with a beautiful two-way friendship — is to get in the right headspace. A real, live puppy is not going to fit neatly into your regular pre-puppy life, and trying to make it so is a recipe for constant angst. The happiest puppy people are the ones who dive into this phase and back-burner their other things. If you need a convincing reason to do that — because it feels wrong to prioritize a little ball of fluff — try this:

Just a baby!
Kidnapped!
From another planet!
Far away from its own kind, its own customs.

Lead with the empathy this idea demands, and you'll find your groove. When you adjust your expectations for this little puppy to where they should be, suddenly training is simple. Not easy, but simple.

Frustration Blocks Problem-Solving

The "poor baby" bit may sound ridiculous to you if you have a new puppy contentedly snoring away in your lap. After all, this pup is lucky to have landed with you. Not only is there plenty of food, but there is an expensive dog bed and an overflowing toy basket. More importantly, you have turned your whole dang life upside-down for this dog. It seems like all you do is deal with the puppy!

All true. But the more relevant truth is this: before you took him home, that eight-week-old puppy spent every single moment of his little life in a cozy, warm scrum with his own tribe. He was cheerily hanging out with his family, doing everything that comes naturally: wrestling, biting, sniffing, chewing, and jumping. He was never alone. He had no idea you were going to swoop in, kidnap him, take him to a new planet, and — here's the kicker — suddenly be mad at him for every behavior that is prized in his culture.

Let that sink in.

Take your time.

Aw, shucks. Now you feel sad. And you want to know what good it does to ponder this depressing thought. After all, this is how it has to go. In our modern society, puppies don't live on Planet Dog forever.

But forcing yourself to rest in this concept increases your empathy for the puppy in front of you. If your mind is focused on your own disappointments (pee on the carpet again! more chewed shoes!), it leads to negative interactions with your puppy that can only hinder progress. If, instead, your mind is filled to the brim with how your poor puppy must be feeling (confused, lonely), your own anger evaporates.

You know what that makes room for? Effective problem-solving.

Oddly enough, the Magic Answer to all of puppyhood is *empathy*. Not some fancy dog-trainer technique. Plain old empathy. I promise it'll make you happier throughout puppyhood, and help you become a dramatically better teacher for your puppy.

Here's a glimpse of what it looks like to approach a handful of the most common puppyhood challenges using Planet Dog empathy. (For more detail on each, see the chapters that follow.)

Biting on Planet Dog

On Planet Dog, everyone in polite society explores new things by mouth. Given the absence of hands, it's the most effective, most satisfying way to engage. Puppies, in particular, use their mouths to play with their friends and to investigate the world around them.

People who aren't thinking about their puppy's natural Planet Dog culture are alarmed by this mouthiness. They feel they may have picked "the wrong one." The kids cry, "I don't like her! She's biting me!" The humans put the pup in the crate for yet another hour, thinking, "That'll teach her."

It doesn't need to be this way.

Owners who are operating out of Planet Dog empathy will wake up in the morning to a bitey pup, and their first thought will be, "Oh! You're missing playing with your friends the way you used to! You're trying to play with us that way!" The thinking cap goes on, and the mind is open. As your pup's only guide to Planet Human, how can you help this dear toddler who's trying her best to navigate a challenging transition? Suddenly the answers are obvious. (For details, see chapter 7.)

So often, particularly regarding mouthiness, people tell me their puppy "just doesn't understand the word *no*." My answer is that when you set up your puppy's day to match her needs, you'll barely need to use that word. Saying "No!" a lot means you may have forgotten that you — say it with me — "Kidnapped! A baby! From another planet!" Having taken that dramatic action, it's only right to do everything you can to help her adjust.

Aloneness on Planet Dog

On Planet Dog, puppies are virtually never alone. From the moment they are born, they are surrounded by littermates and within a leap or two of their mom. That makes for constant companionship, fun, exercise, and warmth.

Once brought to Planet Human, a puppy might spend the vast majority of his time alone in a cold crate in an empty kitchen. When this toddler naturally cries out for companionship, he is yelled at by the human who is his sole connection in this new life. "He needs to learn. He already had a walk around the block, plus I just played with him for a while. Now I'm busy."

There's a better way.

Leading with empathy makes us realize that while eventually this baby needs to learn to hang out alone, shock treatment is not the most effective learning experience. Furthermore, it can easily have the unintended consequence of making it even scarier to be alone. Once inside your puppy's head, you'll gravitate toward a stair-step approach to help him learn to feel content while alone. (For details, see chapter 9.)

As our little alien gets used to life with humans over the first weeks — aided by Planet Dog–oriented approaches — pretty soon puppy is happily enjoying his own company for reasonable stretches of the day that can get longer every week.

The Leash on Planet Dog

On Planet Dog, there are no leashes. Imagine a recently kidnapped puppy's terror when a strange thing is tightened around her neck and suddenly she is pulled around by it. Even worse, she is dragged outside into a world she's never seen before, with loud noises and other creatures that are utterly foreign.

So many new owners are mystified when this pup is reluctant. They just pull her along, thinking, "She's so weird! All dogs like walks. I'm sure she'll get used to it." And generally, she does — but only after experiencing a lot of fear and losing trust in her human.

In contrast, the owner who remembers the key information — "Just a baby!" — will consider how terrifying this could be, which opens up the mind. "Hmm, how could this leash walk be made less frightening?" Ideas abound. (See chapter 8.)

Within days, this pup raised in empathy is happily walking on leash up and down the street with her trusted owner, who feels all the closer to her pup for the journey they've just taken. (The other type of owner, who was in a rush to get these walks going, is still dealing with a skittish walker weeks later.)

Tinkling on Planet Dog

The challenge of potty training is the primary source of the sleepless "What have I done?" nights many new owners experience. Even the most committed humans seem to buckle at the three-week mark and confess to yelling.

Alas, our little kidnapped baby may have just learned, from that angry shout, that her person is unpredictable. As she tries her best to figure out Planet Human, she may also have concluded in that moment:

- I'd better hide from a human if I need to pee! Maybe here behind the couch.

- I don't ever want to pee in front of a human, so I won't pee on leash anymore.

- Right before my person yelled I was looking at the small child, so that must be a bad thing on this planet. I will run from small children now!

Our human potty-training rules make very little sense to those from Planet Dog. While it is obvious to you that the dining-room carpet is no place to relieve yourself, to your puppy it seems ideal: it's away from the prime living space, and it's got nice absorption, plus traction. Start with empathy, understand that your pup has drastically different instincts from yours, and set him up for success. (For details, turn to chapter 6.)

There are no shortcuts. I'd sugarcoat it for you, but that doesn't do you any good in the long run. The kindest thing I can do is give you the truth: after a few days of adjusting, every "accident" is the human's fault. The upside? That means the process is under your control.

The Dream Is within Reach

Frustrated new puppy owners think they're not asking much. "Sheesh, I just want to hang out with him and cuddle." But that's not actually true. We're also asking our puppies not to bark, jump, bite, pee, sniff, or chew. Sometimes it's as if we're asking them not to be dogs.

It is frankly amazing to me how well most puppies do during this shocking transition from one planet to another. They are so adaptable that even when shoehorned immediately into a human's world of repeated "No's," they often do okay.

But in the homes where Planet Dog empathy rules from day 1? Those are the homes where the whole puppyhood thing looks just like it does in the storybooks. Sure, some human priorities were moved to the back burner for six months. But there was no tossing and turning, and there were no secret thoughts of regret. These are the folks who wonder what they did before they got this new friend. They are also, by the way, the people whose dog is walking at a relaxed pace beside them, on a loose leash, gazing up at them from time to time wondering what happy adventure might be coming next.

PART 1

NESTING

1

YOUR MINDSET

Choose to Love This Moment

It's the first day.

That tiny, miraculous ball of fur is curled up, sound asleep, in your lap. Your people are gathered round. You didn't know your home could feel this cozy. You're whispering and grinning at each other. Nobody's looking at a screen. Nobody's even thinking about leaving the room.

Welcome to puppyhood! There are some moments in life that live up to the hype, and the first nap is one of them.

There will be people who tell you you're nuts to have done this. Lots of them. They'll tell you they did puppyhood once and vowed never, ever again. They'll tell you you'll be trapped at home, your life will no longer be your own, and your stuff will be destroyed.

They're not entirely wrong.

Puppyhood *is* intense. There's no such thing as just adding a puppy into the mix and carrying on. Life as you know it is over for now. You're suddenly going to be aware of just how much free time you used to have, and you'll reminisce about how luxurious it was to be able to just *leave things out* around the house.

And yet. There was a reason you reached for puppyhood. Yes, it is the giant disruption the naysayers describe. But who says that's necessarily a bad thing?

For some of us — and this is my fondest hope for you — it turns out that once you temporarily back-burner part of your life to make way for the puppy, your front burner starts to overflow with things that bring happier days, a more relaxed psyche, and a more hopeful window on the world. One of the unexpected outcomes of puppyhood can be a permanent rearrangement of the burners.

As you embark on this adventure, know that the very same puppy in the very same household can create two extremes of experience for a human. The difference is in your own mindset.

You can choose to take a deep breath, be ready, and love this moment.

2

YOUR VILLAGE

Build It Beforehand

At some point in the first month of puppyhood, there's going to be something that feels like an emergency. Maybe:

- you think the puppy may have eaten a rock but you're not sure
- she's terrified of the leash, but that's the only way you can take her outside to pee
- you need to leave town for the weekend because your mom just broke her ankle

When that moment comes, who are you going to call?

Having a great village really helps when you're raising a puppy. Yours will grow organically over time, but it's smart to start putting together your team even before the puppy comes home. Let's build your village.

The Vet

Many folks are surprised when they call the vet to arrange their puppy's first visit, only to find there's a two-week wait for new appointments: "Darn it! That third puppy shot is due tomorrow!" They hurriedly call around and end up at the first vet who has an open slot.

That's not the ideal way to pick the person who's going to guide you for a dozen years in the healthcare of this new little family member. Instead, talk to local friends before you get your puppy. Which vet do the best dog people around you go to, and why?

In larger practices, there may be one vet everybody adores, another who's brand-new, and another who's hard to talk to. It took me years to realize that I should ask for my favorite vet every time I made an appointment. It's so valuable to build a relationship of trust and communication over the years. If you switch around every time, you'll never get there.

Remember that you'll also need an emergency vet who's open 24/7. You may never actually have to use them, but if that 3 a.m. emergency comes, you don't want to be wondering where to go. Put that phone number on your fridge. (Always try to call first, or on the way, when you have to take your dog in.)

A last word on vet selection: I caution you about using cost as your key differentiator. Is that because I'm an out-of-touch billionaire? (Ha! Nope.) It's because the apples-to-apples costs are typically very similar, and when they're not, it's often because a clinic is offering something extra I want, once I know what it is. A vet with a reputation for being "too expensive" may have more sophisticated diagnostic equipment right in the office or might be trained in newer, more effective treatment options. Maybe they insist on higher qualifications for their nurses and techs, which you might not notice but will result in better care. Perhaps the clinic has spent the time and money to train all staff in fear-free techniques, which will help your dog feel more relaxed in that back room. To my mind, those vets aren't really more expensive; they're actually offering a better experience for me and my dog. It might even be cheaper in the long run. For example, you can treat some ear infections with a medication the vet basically paints onto the ear one time, versus the "cheaper" option of you cleaning your dog's painful ear and administering meds twice a day — which is more difficult to do well and may necessitate a follow-up appointment.

My point is this: empower yourself by asking good questions. Vets have no idea how much an individual owner knows or doesn't know. If you're not sure why an expensive option is recommended, ask for more information. Listen to answers about whether there's a less expensive alternative, and what the downsides to that would be. Open up that communication channel, so that you can head out the door understanding exactly why you and your vet chose that treatment path.

Great veterinary care is important, and it will feel expensive if you haven't planned appropriately for it. Opting for pet insurance is often a smart decision.

The Trainer

When you have your first question about your puppy's behavior, you'll be tempted to google it. If you do, you'll get conflicting answers from "experts." Some of the advice out there is great. And some is so damaging that my stomach twists whenever a new client says, "Well, I looked up what to do about the barking on the internet, and they said…"

Instead of typing that question into the search bar and looking at random hits, find a few trusted resources ahead of time, and turn to them whenever you have questions.

- Get a book by a force-free trainer who teaches a positive, relationship-based approach rather than one rooted in dominance and "corrections." (Oh, wait, you already did. Great job!)

- Get a second one, because two excellent training voices are better than one. The classic *Puppy Primer* by Patricia McConnell and Brenda Scidmore is a fantastic choice that offers an easy-to-follow week-by-week training plan. (For more, see Recommendations and Resources at the end of this book.)

- Research local trainers. Look for official credentials (like CPDT, KPA, or PMCT) that offer evidence of experience and expertise. An FDM (family dog mediator) designation is a great sign, too. Remember that this industry is unregulated, and absolutely anyone can call themselves a dog trainer. Super important: if someone is promising quick fixes and a perfect puppy, run.

- Once you've chosen a trainer, arrange for an at-home visit during the first two weeks after your pup comes home. You're going to have a million questions, and having somebody look at your setup and get you on the right road quickly is incredibly helpful. (A Zoom consultation is a close second.) I'd say that 85 percent of the time, we trainers get the first call from a client when the puppy is eight months old and there are "suddenly" a lot of issues. If those folks had struck up a relationship with a trainer at the beginning, they'd have been able to skip some challenges.

- Well-run, safe puppy classes can be wonderful. If you can walk by and observe a class with the instructor beforehand, do it. The vibe should be fun preschool, not military academy. Look for lots of treat pouches.

The Neighbors

The first months of caring for a puppy can make you feel trapped at home. Each social invitation prompts a calculation about just how long you feel you can be away from the puppy at this stage. Before accepting your fate as a prisoner, consider whether there might be a happy solution right up your street.

Puppies benefit enormously from interacting with lots of nice humans — and humans benefit tremendously from a dose of puppy joy. Is there a teenager in the neighborhood who'd love to come over every day at a certain time to play with the puppy out in the yard? How about an elderly neighbor who might enjoy puppy contact? Maybe a home-schooling family one street over would love to work puppy visits into a unit on animal care.

It can feel intimidating and a little awkward to seek out this kind of arrangement. Then there's the question of whether you should offer to pay. The answer is yes, even if they try to refuse to accept it. This kind of money is a drop in the bucket of lifetime dog expenses, and the goodwill that results from making helpers feel appreciated rather than taken for granted is gigantic.

So give visits from neighbors a try, even if it's just for the first two weeks when the pup is neediest. You may find nobody wants it to end, and you'll have neighbors offering to pet sit their favorite doggy whenever you go away.

Pet Sitters and Kennels

Who's the most beloved pet sitter in your area? Don't know? Find out! Even if you don't plan to travel in the first few months, an emergency may come up. If it does, you may be dismayed to find that you're out of luck at boarding kennels because:

- your pup isn't old enough to have had all her distemper-parvovirus shots and is therefore at risk of infection.

- you thought your puppy didn't need the Bordetella (kennel cough) shot, but the kennel requires it ten days before boarding, and now it's too late.

- your pup is seven months old and not yet spayed because the vet advised waiting until after her first heat — which means the kennel can't take her.

When people face this last-minute dilemma, they often turn to Rover.com, or a more local pet-sitting service, to find somebody who will come and stay at their home. That can be just fine, but it can also feel very uncomfortable to hand over your keys to a complete stranger as you head out the door. It feels much better to have compiled a list of pet sitters that folks in your area trust. Puppies are darling, but they're hard work. Be prepared to pay for great care.

3

YOUR SETUP

Create a Puppy Apartment

Want your puppy to seem brilliant? Limit her choices by providing a well-designed puppy space. She'll stun you with how "good" she is.

Every now and then our adopters just rave about the "supersmart" foster puppy they just picked up from us. "Oh my gosh, I think she was potty trained in a day!" "Seriously, she's never chewed the furniture." I'm delighted, and I ask them to show me their setup. Inevitably, I see a wonderful little Puppy Apartment within the main living area. Bingo. Great job. Creating the right initial space for your pup can save your sanity, save your stuff, save on emergency vet bills, and save your puppy's learning experience by limiting her ability to make mistakes.

Whatever you do, do not let a new puppy have the run of the house. None of us has the bandwidth to supervise every single second, so if a puppy is given a whole-house pass, inevitably there are tinkles that teach the pup it's fine to pee inside; sofa-chewing episodes that teach the pup that it's a really satisfying activity; and the swallowing of an unmentionable item from the bathroom trash that necessitates a scary trip to the vet.

All. Completely. Unnecessary.

Just create a Puppy Apartment. What exactly it looks like, how long you use it, and how it expands over time will vary, but the bottom line is that you need to limit the puppy's space. The wonderful animal behaviorist Kathy Sdao would call this an instance of being a "choice architect" for your dog — helping your pup practice making good choices because you haven't put any bad ones on the table.

Think Small and Central

Your Puppy Apartment will be a puppy-proofed space in the main living area that ideally has:

1. you happily hanging out in or near it a lot;

2. easy access to the puppy's outdoor bathroom area; and

3. no carpet.

This might be your whole kitchen, or perhaps a portion of your family room with the rugs rolled up. It is absolutely *not* an isolated bedroom, basement, or laundry room. The puppy needs to be with people! First of all, she misses her littermates. In addition to meeting her need for company, having her in the middle of things allows her to learn and get used to the sights, sounds, and smells of Planet Human. Right now she's like a sponge in her ability to soak up new information. Let's put her where there are good things to absorb.

Equipment

You'll likely need to use gates or linkable exercise pens to build your Puppy Apartment. Sure, that equipment is ugly, but so is your mood when your carpet is ruined and your new shoes destroyed. Keep in mind this phase will pass. One day your home can return to its former aesthetic glory. For now your priority is setting your puppy up for success.

Next comes a crate, soft bedding, food and water bowls, and toys, toys, toys. (For recommendations, see PuppyPicks.com.)

Think about borrowing some of these items before getting drawn in by all the products that will be calling your name once you start searching online. Your needs will evolve quickly as the puppy grows. The setup that's ideal for a nine-week-old pup may be knocked down or jumped over by that same pup two weeks later. So don't get too heavily invested — either emotionally or financially — but limit the pup's space for at least the first few weeks, and probably months.

I'm often asked about puppy pee pads. Believe me, I understand the appeal. But by the time your pup comes home with you at eight weeks or older, he's ready to learn to potty outside. If you put down scented pads that actually encourage peeing indoors, you're setting back your puppy's learning. Instead of inadvertently teaching your puppy to pee on the floor, put your effort into making darn sure your puppy is outside often enough that your floors stay clean.

Access to the Outdoors

A lightning-fast route to the outdoor potty area is a giant bonus for a Puppy Apartment, because that trip is going to happen every half hour at first. The longer the trek to the door, the more likely there'll be an accident along the way. The easier you make this process on yourself, the more likely you will do it right, which is what makes the difference between a puppy who's potty trained quickly and one who takes forever.

As long as we're on the subject, if it is in any way possible for you, a fenced yard is a dream during the potty-training weeks. Eliminating the extra hassle of putting on a harness and a leash — with a puppy who is used to neither — is life-changing. A physical fence also facilitates great free play and natural exploration, in addition to allowing doggy playdates.

It's okay if you're in an apartment, or renting with zero ability to alter the yard — you'll make do. But if you can build a fence, don't postpone the decision. "We'll get it later if we need it," some new puppy owners tell me. That's when I start to beg and plead. Nobody ever regrets fencing the yard for a dog. Instead I often hear, "I can't imagine how much harder puppyhood would have been without the fence."

If a fence truly isn't in the cards, think about setting up a temporary one using options from your local home improvement store. (They have everything from ugly orange snow fencing to pretty wrought-iron-style offerings.) For a while at least, your pup is going to be small enough that this kind of temporary enclosure will keep her safe, and it will make your potty-training experience a thousand times easier.

PART 2

THE FIRST
WEEK

4

THE FIRST DAY

Keep It Simple

For most puppy-parents-to-be, some daydreaming takes place as the big day approaches. Folks tend to spend time imagining the smiles on their kids' faces ("Should we make a TikTok, honey?") or planning to have the neighbors over for pizza to celebrate. Just as brides get carried away with wedding thoughts instead of marriage thoughts, people getting a puppy sometimes get pulled away from the puppy itself and into the event.

But that's not you.

Instead, as that big day approaches, you're going to think with compassion about your new puppy. You'll urge your whole household to ponder what this puppy is going to be feeling and thinking. With that consideration always top of mind, you can plan a great first day.

The Timing

If possible, bring home a puppy at the beginning of a three-day stretch when you know you'll be able to devote a lot of time and bandwidth to this darling little project. Ideally, it'll be a time frame when some extra hands are available.

- Maybe that's a Friday afternoon, if you're a family with two working adults and some teenagers.

- Maybe it's a Monday, if you're a family with school-age kids. That can make for a calmer first week, as you and the puppy get to know each other while the littlest "helpers" are in school.

- If you're empty nesters who work from home, the best stretch of time is one when neither of you has a huge presentation, a deadline, or travel.
- If you're single, it might be a weekend when your best friend can sleep over.

Whatever your situation, I like to see a pup arrive at his new home by midafternoon. The first night can be tough, and the more time a puppy has to get used to his new environment and to feel safe with his new people, the more likely he'll be able to settle down and sleep.

The Drive

You'll probably be picking up your puppy in a car. Please get a co-pilot. It is terribly difficult to drive *and* to appreciate how cute your puppy is at the same time. You need a trusted human with a cozy lap to ride shotgun. That person will prevent the puppy from crawling onto your steering wheel or down to the pedals, so they'll keep you and everyone else on the road safe.

It's smart to bring a small crate or a kitty carrier along as well. (Borrow from neighbors. I promise there are a dozen sitting in dusty closets on your street.) While many pups just nap the whole way home, others may be difficult to contain. Being able to confine them easily is a lifesaver.

If your puppy comes from a really good breeder or foster home, it's possible that he's already a pro at being in a crate and at car rides. But most pups have not had those experiences yet, and your puppy is likely to cry. He may also throw up out of a mixture of motion sickness and anxiety. Bring a towel and maybe some pet wipes for safe cleanup.

Distractions for the ride — a bully stick, a squeaky toy, a

Snuggle Puppy — might be just what your puppy needs to take his mind off the highly unusual day he's having.

Planning a Low-Key Welcome

Please don't make ambitious plans for your puppy's arrival. This has already been the biggest, most challenging day of his life: he's left his family and gone on a huge adventure with strangers. I know you love him already, but you need to give him a second to catch up and love you back.

A special note on surprises: promise me you will not put the puppy in a closed box and then do a big designed-for-social-media reveal that produces squeals from small humans or freaky behavior from an older dog. If the puppy is a surprise for the kids, you can have the same fun by putting dog toys in that box instead of a puppy, and doing it the day before the puppy arrives. Let the kids scream and squeal and get it all out of their systems. Then explain to them exactly why you did it this way: "This is just a baby doggy, and we don't want to scare him." Ask the kids to imagine they're that puppy, and think about what behavior from kids might make them feel worried versus safe and content.

What to Do First

The moment you get home and open the car door, it is only fitting that the next move is a potty break. (Welcome to your new life.) Take the puppy straight to the grass and encourage him to walk around (get down low, use a cheery voice) until you have success. This is when a fence is ideal, because using this huge moment to also introduce a leash and a collar can set you back on all fronts.

Next, head inside to the Puppy Apartment. Show him where his water is and offer a little bowl of kibble, even if it isn't mealtime yet. Ideally you've brought something from his previous home — maybe a blanket — with the scent of his littermates. Put that in the bed, which you've perhaps placed in the open crate. Hang out, talk to him, and sit on the floor so he can come over to you if he wants. Thirty minutes later, head back outside to the same spot where he peed before, and walk and play until that happens again. Tell him, "Yesss! What a good puppy."

Introductions and Visitors

Ponder the timing of your various introductions. Remember, the pup has a lot to take in at once. If you have other pets, you might want to let him get used to all the new humans, and to the new Puppy Apartment, for a few hours before introducing your adult dog or your cats. (See part 3 for help on introducing housemates.)

And what if your friends and neighbors are clamoring to come meet the new addition? It's wonderful if you have a big, enthusiastic village, but try to arrange for these welcomes to happen in small, short encounters over the first week. Calm guests are awesome for a new puppy, but crowds can be overwhelming.

Follow the Puppy's Lead

For the next few hours you will be dying to interact with the puppy. If he is all waggy and eager and pushing to investigate new people and new toys, wonderful! Follow that lead.

But if your puppy just keeps napping? That's 100 percent normal, and you want to follow that lead, too. Just settle down nearby — chatting, reading, watching a movie — and wait for him to wake up in his own time. All puppies need a lot of sleep, and puppies who've just entered a new world sometimes need much more. Don't worry — he'll be perky soon enough! (Heh heh heh. You may look back with nostalgia at this peaceful time.)

5

SLEEPING ARRANGEMENTS

Yes, You Can Sleep with Your New Puppy

I can't even tell you how many times I've heard a new client confess: "I know it's wrong, but we allowed the puppy to sleep with us last night. I've read about how I must crate him. But he was crying. He just seemed so sad. And when we took him in bed with us, he settled right down, and I finally got some sleep. Now what?"

Almost every new puppy owner I counsel has searched dog training websites and encountered the following stern rule:

> Crate your new eight-week-old puppy at night. You'll have to get up once or twice to let them out to go to the bathroom, but put them right back in. Ignore them when they cry. They'll get used to it.

If you have followed that advice and it's working beautifully for you...okay! Happy trails. You can skip this chapter.

If, however, this approach feels wrong to you, and you are dying to soothe your crying new puppy, I'd like to give you permission to listen to your gut and create a softer alternative for those first few nights. In fact, here's the shocking advice I give to clients: if you want to, go ahead and bring that pup into bed with you. It's what we do at our house, and here's why.

How Puppies Sleep

We have now fostered well over two hundred puppies, mostly moms with their litters. I spend countless hours watching the way puppies

25

sleep, and I can tell you this: it is almost never alone. It is in a warm, snuggled, co-breathing, ever-shifting pile of the beings they know and love best. There are puppy sighs, and, as they stretch, the sweetest little groans. Sometimes somebody staggers away to find a cooler spot, but an hour later they're back, burrowing into a nook between their sister's head and their brother's butt. It is clearly bliss.

Then one day, after two months spent sleeping exactly in this manner, the puppy goes "home" with his new humans. They are kind and responsible, and they are simply trying to follow expert advice when they take that confused puppy and stick him into a crate, alone, for hours, at night, with nothing to distract him. The puppy has nothing to do but miss his (real) family.

Of *course* he cries.

It is not the end of the world. Eventually (probably) he will get over it. It might be in an hour, or a week, but eventually (probably) the puppy does sleep alone in the crate without crying. The crate-them-right-away approach works fine for many, but for some pups it creates such terror that they develop separation anxiety. There are other, more empathetic options.

Benefits of Co-sleeping

At our house, when we have a pup just separated from the litter, we don't do the alone-in-the-crate-all-night thing. Instead, we do our best to recreate that puppy pile she's used to, right in our own bed. We pop that puppy in between us. After a very confusing first day without the comfort of her original pack, you can almost feel the puppy sighing in relief, thinking, "Okay, now this feels right."

There is no crying, which means we get lots more sleep. Sure, we wake from time to time when the puppy readjusts, burrows in under an arm, perhaps licks a face. But seriously? Those moments are delicious. If you are inclined to love that, don't let that stern internet advice deprive you of one of the sweetest times in the world. Life's short. Let yourself have the 3 a.m. puppy snuggle.

In this early phase, your days will be filled with puppy management and potty training. Sometimes that's not very relaxing. But this? For some of us, it's a giant destresser. Treat yourself, and your puppy, to six hours of easy bonding at night. You may find that it advances your daytime interactions too.

Won't My Puppy Pee in My Bed? Or Fall Off?

A big objection to co-sleeping is that everyone's sure the puppy will pee in the bed. After all, when folks using a crate take the crying puppy out at 2 a.m., she always pees. They conclude that she was crying because she needed to go out. Maybe. But more likely she was crying because she was sad and lonely, and she can easily hold it from 11 p.m. to 5 a.m.

How do I know? Because we do it all the time. With us, eight-week-old pups sleep soundly for those six hours with no bathroom break — happily snuggled into a family pile. Here's how to make that more likely:

1. Give no food after 7 p.m.

2. Offer no water after 8:30 p.m. (Maybe a sip, but no big glugs.)

3. Have a long, frisky play session outside just before bed. Not a quick step outside for a little pee, but a nice, motion-filled adventure. (Motion encourages pees and poops.)

When we follow those rules, the puppies do not have to go out in the middle of the night. The bed itself can work a bit like a crate, in that it is a clearly defined space where the puppy is "living" for the moment. Pups don't like to pee where they live. If instead I were sleeping on the floor in a sleeping bag, letting the pup nestle in with me there, that pup would at some point during the night walk over to a far corner of the room and pee, because he might as well — it's easy. But up on a big bed where he isn't quite sure how to get down, a shuffling puppy will just settle back down to sleep.

Mind you, once the pup truly awakens in the morning —
not just shifting for comfort, but alert and walking around on the
bed — it is time to leap into action. A delay could make the pup
feel desperate and try to get off the bed (dangerous if your bed is
high), or just go ahead and pee. Jump out of bed — there's no time
for your own bathroom break! — pick up that puppy, and carry him
outside. Whatever you do, don't make the puppy walk to the door,
because the motion of walking will mean "game over." Carry the
pup to the outdoor potty area and then be ready to reward her for
what will naturally and quickly follow.

My Puppy Won't Settle Down

If you plan to have your pup sleep in bed with you, introduce her to
the spot well before you expect her to settle down. If you don't, of
course the pup will be filled with questions — "A new place! What
happens here? What do I smell?" — and nobody will be going to
sleep anytime soon.

Just take the pup up into the bedroom a few times during the
day ahead of bedtime. Let her explore the place a bit and hang out
on the bed, maybe chewing a toy as you supervise. This will demy-
stify the bedroom and the bed, so that when pup comes back up at
11 p.m., appropriate lights-out behavior is more likely.

Speaking of which, turn out the lights and stop talking. Be
boring. If pup has had a long day and plenty of interaction, five
minutes of quiet time in the darkness, with maybe a little chew toy,
should see the pup giving in to sleep with a sigh and a snuggle.

But I Don't Want to Sleep with a Grown Dog!

Often folks are open to the idea of sleeping with a little puppy, but
the idea of sharing the bed with a seventy-pound grown dog is a
hard no. They worry that once the habit is established, there's no
going back.

Not true. You can create a plan to transition the pup to the crate, either in a few days or a few weeks. By then, two important things will have happened:

1. Your pup will be happy at your house, understanding that you're her new family.

2. If you have accustomed the pup to her crate with positive sessions during the daytime, she'll be used to napping alone in there, and sleeping there at night will not be a big stretch. To make it easier, place an extra crate next to your bed, start using that every now and then during the day, and then one night — after a particularly adventurous, exhausting day — pop her in there to sleep at night.

Perhaps you're thinking, If she's going to be sleeping alone in her crate soon, why not just bite the bullet and do it from the get-go? My answer is just...empathy. Surely you remember sad, lonely, and fearful moments of your life. Just because things turned out okay doesn't mean those moments weren't horrible for you. So why not keep your puppy from having that experience if you possibly can? Just because *you* know it's all going to be okay doesn't mean the puppy does. When it comes to a very long night spent alone just when the puppy has gone through the most shocking transition of her life, I'm going to err on the side of emotional comfort.

6

POTTY TRAINING

Focus Now, So Your Puppy Can Learn Fast

Potty training a puppy sounds so deceptively simple: Just take your eight-week-old pup outside every half hour, so that she'll have a chance to go in the right spot. She'll never have a chance to make a mistake. Soon enough, it'll be an ingrained habit, and she'd never think of relieving herself inside.

Heh heh heh.

If only "soon enough" were one week. The truth is that for the bleary-eyed new puppy owner, just that week of outings every thirty minutes can feel like a century. Even the most enthusiastic, committed folks seem to buckle at the three-week mark. They can't believe the pup still needs this level of oversight, so they start to relax. The tight oversight slackens. Half an hour stretches to an hour and a half. Inevitably, there is an accident. Then a few more. Finally, even from the nicest folks, there is yelling.

That outburst — however understandable — has an unfortunate impact on our kidnapped puppy. It erodes her trust. Instead of being the puppy's rock in this strange new land, her person is now yet another unpredictable source of confusion. As she processes this moment, she may also conclude:

- I'd better sneak away from a human if I need to pee! Maybe I'll go here behind the desk.

- Since it's scary to pee near humans, I won't pee when I'm on leash.

- When my person yelled I was looking at the neighbor's dog out the window, so that must be a bad thing on this planet. I will bark at other dogs now!

What she almost certainly did *not* learn from that moment was the intended lesson: pee outside only. Our human potty-training rules make very little sense to the folks from Planet Dog. While it is obvious to you that the dining room carpet is no place to relieve yourself, to your puppy it seems ideal: it's away from the prime living space, and it's got nice absorption, plus traction. So. Start with empathy, understand that your pup has drastically different instincts from yours, and set her up for success.

Here's how:

- Limit her space to one puppy-friendly room at first — perhaps the kitchen or family room. Ideally this Puppy Apartment is a spot with no carpet and quick access to the outdoor potty area.

- Gates, pens, and crates are your friends. Use them to set your pup up to learn. Giving a pup freedom to roam around the house sounds nice, but it isn't, because it only leads to accidents.

- The human "on duty" must get that pup outside, and walking around, once every half hour to start. Only with complete success can that stretch to forty-five minutes, then an hour.

- Keep eyes on that puppy 100 percent of the time she's not in a crate. Note for less enthusiastic family members: "eyes on" does not mean "in room, with laptop open." Learn the signals that mean she's about to go (abruptly walking to a corner? sniffing the ground?) and respond immediately by distracting her with a clap and cheerily sweeping her up and out, where you can praise her for doing the right thing.

Ready to hear the hard part? There are no shortcuts. I'd sugar-coat it for you, but that doesn't do you any good in the long run, so here it is: every "accident" is the human's fault.

"Hey! Where's the empathy for the human?" I promise, I do feel that! But you'll get that elsewhere when you talk to other people who can't believe you actually got a puppy. I'm here to speak for the puppy, who did not choose to be kidnapped by aliens who thought they could carry on their regular day-to-day routine afterward.

Hang in there! This too shall pass. If you stay patient, you'll be done potty training before you know it.

7

PUPPY BITING

Survive Sharp Teeth by Planning for Them

Puppies bite. Every single one of them. Sure, the degree varies, but biting is a fundamental part of how puppies interact with the world. They bite to play; they bite to investigate. They bite because they're full of energy; they bite because they're overtired. They bite because they're teething; and sometimes they bite when teething is supposedly over.

Puppy biting is the most natural thing on Planet Dog. Unfortunately, we humans aren't equipped with the furry coat that would protect us from those sharp puppy teeth. That's why we need to have a plan that includes:

- anticipating and meeting the puppy's natural needs
- keeping a rotating selection of tug toys within arm's reach
- having a jar of treats ready to help teach and reward behavior that works on Planet Human
- setting up an easy escape from the biting by using gates or pens
- keeping a selection of long-lasting chews

Of course, it's terrible for you when it seems your puppy is attacking everybody. But that's nothing compared to the sadness of being a misunderstood puppy, kidnapped and taken far away from his own kind. When it comes to puppy biting, there's no reason to

be unprepared, no reason to be surprised, and — most important —
no reason to be mad at the puppy.

Have a plan instead.

Meet Canine Needs First

This first section — on meeting natural canine needs — may strike
you as a detour from the urgent topic at hand: "When the heck is
she going to tell me what to do when my puppy tries to bite me?"
I'll get to that, I promise. But listen up: this subhead is almost the
whole shebang. Do this part well, and it'll be easy to use the tips in
the following sections to manage biting in the moment. If you skip
this seemingly unrelated part, you'll be facing an uphill battle.

How do I know? Because exasperated owners drop their puppies off at my house, saying they can barely interact with their pup
because of the nonstop biting. Hours later, when I send them videos of the puppy here — interacting with us beautifully, with zero
biting — they are simultaneously very hopeful and pretty annoyed.
It's like when you bring the car to the repair shop and it won't make
that weird noise anymore.

I can't explain the car thing, but I certainly know what's happening at our house. I jump into meeting the puppy's Planet Dog
needs before I try to interact in a human-oriented manner. At our
house a puppy gets to frolic — teeth and all — with fellow canines,
sniff around in a yard bursting with interesting scents, dig in some
dirt, chew some sticks, and maybe bark at a deer or a fox.

When the puppy has had maybe half an hour of all that and
wanders over to me, he's no longer full of the wild energy of a puppy
who's been trapped in a pen in the living room. It's not that the
puppy is exhausted after his half hour with us; he is simply filled up
with appropriate experiences. He's like a calmly alert second-grade
boy who just had an awesome time at recess and is now actually able
to sit down at his desk and listen a bit.

No matter where or how you live, you can find a way to give
your puppy daily doses of being a real dog. You'll get the biggest

bang for your buck by finding a puppy friend right in the neighborhood for regular, delightfully bitey playdates. But an unrushed "sniffari" in an interesting spot, some interaction with nice adult dogs, and plenty of chances to chew or dig will help, too. Do these things, and watch the biting diminish naturally.

Okay, *now* it's time to get to the in-the-biting-moment strategies. But just remember: every time you're struggling to get them to work, ask yourself, "Did my puppy get to be a dog much today?" If the answer is no, start there.

Use Toys to Fend Off, Then Teach Tug

With those sharp teeth and the clever disguise of extreme cuteness, it takes only a second for a puppy to draw blood or rip your pants. And believe it or not, the worst part of these episodes isn't the blood or the rip — it's the fact that your puppy got a chance to rehearse that bitey behavior. Chances are it felt fun and rewarding to her — "Yay! This feels like being back with my littermates!" — which means she's more likely to repeat it.

Don't let that happen. Instead, every single time you approach, reach into the overflowing toy basket you have handily placed right at the entrance to every place where the puppy spends time. Grab a tug toy or two. At first, when the puppy is brand-new to you, you're using those toys to fend her off. But soon enough you'll be encouraging a game of Tug.

Tug is a beautiful compromise between Planet Dog and Planet Human. It allows us to give the puppy a "Yes" in response to her innate impulse for physical, bitey play — instead of trying to shut her down with a "No" that's as ineffective as it is unfair. (After all, we kidnapped her from Planet Dog.)

Back in the dominance-obsessed dark ages of dog training, "experts" used to tell folks that playing Tug would teach their dog to question their authority. The modern, happy reality is that Tug can be a great opportunity to build cooperative communication, as you gradually add structure to the game. For example, you begin to teach that a polite Sit restarts the game, and you work toward teaching the puppy to Drop the toy. The result? Fun, learning, communication, and bonding.

Of course, if you leave nice smelly dish towels and dirty laundry around where the puppy can grab them, he'll assume they're fair game for Tug. Here's what to do when that happens:

1. Ignore the item instead of chasing the puppy around and unintentionally confirming that it's playtime.

2. Distract the pup with a new activity while somebody else retrieves that item.

3. Use this as a helpful reminder not to leave that stuff in reach.

Toys: Which Ones, and Where

How well the replace-hands-with-toy strategy works depends on your toy skills. Choosing the right toys, observing closely which ones are favorites for your particular pup, and keeping them in critical spots are key talents.

In the earliest fend-off stage, big stuffed animals that block the puppy's mouth and protect your hand are a great choice. As you move into playing Tug, you'll likely find that long, flat, furry toy animals (bonus if there's a squeaker in the tail) work best. As for ropelike toys, the stretchy, soft, braided style (make some yourself out of felt or fleece) tends to work better than the thick, hard ones, which puppies usually ignore.

Keep in mind that length is a hand saver. Skilled puppy wranglers can make good use of a six-inch tug toy, but newbies will find that the longer the toy, the safer the human. Especially if you have young kids, you'll be grateful if you add that three-foot, crinkly snake to the selection.

In addition to choosing the right toys for your individual puppy, the way you store and manage them can make all the difference. Yes, I want you to have so many options that you could cover the puppy's floor with them. But should you? Nope. Because if that toy has been lying around in sight for days, it's not going to be very enticing. If, instead, you select the fluffy, squeaky raccoon the puppy hasn't seen since last Tuesday, bingo! Teeth are engaged in a way that makes everybody happy. Always rotate your toys. Keep just a few out for morning, then swap them out for the afternoon, and again in the evening.

From Tug to Training

In calmer moments, when your puppy is not all teeth, you'll be introducing a fun new way to pass the time: training. By using tiny bits of food to teach and reward behaviors like Sit and Touch, you're opening up a whole new way for the puppy to interact with another being. The more the puppy learns to love that fun, food-filled training, the sooner you can use training as a way to redirect the biting. On hearing your voice, instead of continuing an assault on your pant leg, the pup will learn to stop and think, "Oh, right. Let's do that instead." Win-win.

One of the best training games to play with a jumpy or bitey puppy is trainer Leslie McDevitt's Ping-Pong, an energetic version of Find It that sends dogs back and forth in front of you. Here's how it works: as Pup heads toward you, you toss a treat very obviously on the floor, calling out the cue "Find It!" Pup will gobble it down and then swivel back toward you. As her eyes meet yours, say "Yesss!" and toss a treat to the other side, calling, "Find it!" Repeat, repeat, repeat.

Here are the advantages to this simple game:

- It rewards eye contact and a focus on you (because that's what restarts the game), which is the first step in training.

- It's a very active game for the puppy (so it suits a jumpy or bitey mood), and yet controlled from your perspective (so it suits your desire for minimizing chaos).

- It can be scaled up in terms of difficulty (by throwing the treat farther away), energy expended (by playing from a seated position and adding a little jump over your extended legs), or behavior needed to restart the game (progressing from making eye contact to asking for a Sit and then a Sit-Touch-Spin).

If you greet your bitey pup with a short game of Tug followed by a few minutes of this kind of training, you'll have used up some energy and established an atmosphere of cooperation. Mental stimulation can be more tiring than plain old physical exertion, which is one reason Ping-Pong is better than an endless game of Tug.

This approach won't work on day 1, because you haven't yet built up the understanding that listening to you presents opportunities to earn yummy stuff. Your biting strategy at first is fending off teeth with stuffed animals. You can follow up a few days later by introducing a more nuanced Tug game. It may be a week or more before you can successfully use a training session to deal with a bitey mood.

Walking Away: Pens, Gates, and Crates

Of course, sometimes none of these strategies work. (Remember, that's when you ask yourself, "Oh, wait, has my puppy had a chance to be a dog today?") Even when you're doing everything right, there often comes a witching hour where nobody can be safely around the puppy. This is where the beauty of "management" shines. Say hello to pens, gates, and crates.

Sometimes, we just need to be able to pop the pup into a safe area where she can't do any harm. Use this option when:

- you truly do not have time this morning to give the pup the playdate or sniffari she really needs
- you've been trying Tug and/or training, but pup is still wildly going for your limbs
- the combination of the kids' moods and the puppy's mood bodes disaster

- the puppy is in a wild mood because of being overtired and needs confinement to encourage sleep

To ease the moment of separation, toss a handful of kibble on the floor ("Find It!") and/or use a chew.

Chews: Bones, Bully Sticks, and Kongs

Sometimes, your puppy's biting isn't a quest for engagement but is much simpler: a demonstration of his need to chew. Chewing is a natural canine pastime, and for teething puppies it's vital. Having safe, enticing things on hand that prompt a long, satisfying chew session will pay off by reinforcing the habit of chewing "legal" items.

But what's safe to use? There are horror stories about rawhide chews that cause intestinal blockages, bully sticks that pose a choking hazard, toys with threads that get swallowed and tangle or perforate intestines, and marrow bones that break off and puncture organs. In fact, there's almost no chew item that's completely safe. Just because it's labeled for puppy use doesn't mean it won't land you at the emergency vet.

Still, puppies absolutely need to chew, and those veterinary disasters are highly unlikely. Everybody has to make their own risk-assessment choices. Here are my own guidelines:

- Food dispensers like Kongs and Toppls (in the correct, nonswallowable sizes for your pup) are the safest choices. Put nutritious stuff in there (mostly moistened kibble, with extras like a spoonful of canned food, leftover carrots or beans, plain yogurt, or a smear of peanut butter) so that you'll feel comfortable using these every day. Freeze them so they last twenty minutes instead of five. (If you're thinking that a full Toppl might be almost a whole meal, you're right. So just cut down on the rest of the pup's food for the day.)

- When introducing other chew items, watch like a hawk at first while you're learning your puppy's chewing style, and stay nearby with an ear open.

- As you evaluate your pup's chewing style, watch out for a pup who chews fast and can break off pieces. He'll require a more limited selection of allowed items.

- Keep in mind that the presence of another dog will often make a puppy chew too fast.

- Another cause of dangerous, too-fast chewing is the approach of an owner saying in a threatening tone, "Hey, give that to me." If you need to take something away, stay cheery, pay no attention to the item, and make a little trail of treats in the other direction. As pup follows the fun new yummies, swipe the chew he left behind.

- Fresh marrow bones that your local butcher cuts to about a three-inch length are awesome. While adult dogs can break them into pointy parts or crack their teeth on them, puppies don't have the strength for that. I am happy to leave a puppy unsupervised in a crate with a nice new marrow bone like this. If you want to make that bone last a few days, pop it back in the fridge after each twenty-minute chewing session.

- Rawhides and bully sticks are notorious for causing digestive upset, blockages, and choking problems. You'd think that would mean I'd avoid them, but nope. It just means these are the things I supervise 100 percent of the time. First of all, I only buy the giant sizes, because it's the tiny ones marked "for puppies" that are most likely to get swallowed or lodged. I get the ones that are either super-thick or super-long, and I offer them to pups in twenty-minute increments before I offer a cheery "Trade!," swapping it for a very enticing bite of something followed by a distracting game of Tug or Fetch. The chew goes back in the basket, and I throw it away well before it is chewed to a size that would make it a choking hazard. (Yes, given the price of bully sticks, that kills me, but stomach surgery would cost more.)

Is Your Puppy Overtired?

One final tip for dealing with extreme mouthiness is the easiest one of all: ponder whether your puppy is getting enough rest. Anyone who's had a toddler can grasp the idea that the wild creature in front of you may not be bursting with energy but instead may be overtired. Sometimes the puppies who seem the most bitey are the ones from active households with a lot of people and motion. These pups don't want to miss out, so they jump up from their nap every time they hear a noise. But puppies need enormous amounts of sleep — for the youngest ones, two hours of napping for every hour awake may be the optimal balance.

This multifaceted plan for helping humans cope with puppy biting may look overwhelming on the page. But it's really not! You just need to do two things: (1) meet Planet Dog needs and (2) teach Planet Human ways. Keep those two things always in mind, and you've got the guidance you need.

8

THE LEASH

Why Doesn't My Puppy Want a Walk?

You just brought your new puppy home, and you can't wait to head out on that first walk. You've been picturing this happy moment forever. You pop on the leash, swing open the door, and...your puppy won't move.

Huh.

So you pull her a little, thinking she just has to get into the swing of things. Now she's flat-out refusing. She has planted herself, elbows locked.

Weird.

When you try again later, she gets a whole ten feet down the walkway before the brakes come on. You pick her up and try carrying her a bit. When you set her down, she'll walk all right — straight back to the house, desperately straining the whole way.

If you're like most folks, you're mystified and a little disappointed. Aren't dogs supposed to like walks more than anything else?

It's Sensible Self-Preservation

The truth is, it makes total sense when a puppy is hesitant to head out on a leash with her new owner. As stunned as puppy owners often are at this turn of events, let's look at the experience from the puppy's perspective.

- This first week, your new pup is in a completely new environment without the canine family she's always known.

- Previously, any new experience took place surrounded by

littermates, but she has to process this leash-and-walk thing all alone.

- This may be her first day wearing a collar — a strange thing snug around her neck.

- This may be her first moment with a leash attached to that collar, adding pressure that might make her feel trapped. (Just because we humans are used to seeing dogs on leash does not mean it is natural for *them*.)

- It's possible that her only outdoor time has been spent in the same yard. As you open the door in this new place, she is overwhelmed by strange smells, sounds, and sights. Maybe she's never gone down steps before, or heard a car, or seen a kid on a bike. She needs to process all of that at her own pace.

- As nice as you are, you're still a relative stranger to your puppy, so your presence may not yet be reassuring.

So it's not shocking if a new puppy hates her first walk. In fact, it's more surprising when she doesn't — and it likely means she had a good breeder or foster home where somebody had the time to introduce her gently to new experiences.

But never fear. You'll be happily walking together soon if you follow these steps.

Slow Down the Process

The key is simple: use your own empathy as a guide, and break this overwhelming experience into smaller, digestible pieces.

- Spend the first afternoon with just a light little collar on the pup (not a big heavy leather thing with studs). Distract the pup with fun toys and play so he doesn't just sit around thinking about how itchy and annoying that collar is. It may take minutes, hours, or days to get used to. (Many puppies scratch at that strange-feeling new collar so much the first few days that their owners think they have fleas.)

- Give pup special treats (a bite of turkey or a morsel of cheese) right after you put on the collar, to create a positive association.

- When he's okay with a collar, start attaching a light kitty leash. Let him drag it if that works best. Pick up the end if that works better, but keep it completely slack, with zero neck pressure. Toss treats in front of him and say, "Find It!" to keep him moving forward and not obsessed with biting the leash. The goal is to see from the pup's body language that he's not freaked out by the feeling of the leash.

- Are things going well? Then try all this outside in the yard. Keep tossing those treats out front. Talk in a happy voice, bend your knees, and get your face close as you encourage movement. If pup is hesitant, try combining some dancing steps with a playful voice. You want to signal zero pressure, just an inviting attitude.

- At other times during that day, without the leash if it's a distraction, take baby steps to help him get used to all the new outdoor sights and sounds. Sit together on your front stoop, watching the world go by, talking to him about what he's seeing, and offering a tiny piece of hot dog after trucks, dogs, or kids on skateboards pass.

Getting to this point — a pup who's mellow about walking around the yard with you holding the leash — may take three minutes or three days. However long it takes is just fine.

As for all these fun distractions you've been using to take the pup's mind off the collar and the leash — the bent knees and eye contact, the dancing steps, the clapping hands, the sing-song voice, the treats, plus the lack of pressure in your vibe — bring all of that with you as you take this leash experience on the road.

If you live in a city with no option except a leashed walk for going to the bathroom, this process obviously has to be compressed. Still, an empathetic mindset will help you find ways to make leash introduction more comfortable.

Collar First: Harness Later

You may notice that I keep talking about collars instead of harnesses. Many folks start with a harness because it seems more comfortable or safer, but in my opinion, it just adds to the puppy's reaction of "Oh my gosh, what the heck are you putting on me?" It kills me to watch a new client trying to squish their wriggling puppy into the shiny new harness somebody sold them. I see the human focused on figuring out which buckle goes where, often completely unaware of the terror their puppy is displaying. The final straw for me is seeing that harness sliding all over the place on the poor puppy as we set off for a walk. And although people often feel a harness offers better security, I've known many puppies who've slipped out of those things.

My choice is a martingale collar for the first few walking sessions. It's a collar that has a little loop where the leash is attached, which tightens slightly if the puppy tries to pull on it. A simple buckle collar would have to be tightened too much to be safe on a walk, because puppies can wriggle out of collars surprisingly easily. Sometimes I see a pup hanging out all day in a way-too-tight collar, and it's because her folks want to keep her safe on a walk. Instead, just use a martingale for the walk. It's easy to put on, light to wear, and 100 percent secure. I wait until I've built more confidence with a pup to add the extra hurdle of a harness.

Enlist a Doggy Escort

By far the fastest way to get a puppy to walk forward enthusiastically is to pair her with an experienced furry friend. It is hilarious to watch a pup who was utterly refusing to move suddenly trot off happily the second another dog walks by. If you can scout out a neighbor with a wonderful, calm adult dog, recruit that team to help you with three walks in three days. It's more than likely this escort will be all it takes to convince your pup that it's just fine to be out and about.

Two things to watch out for:

1. Avoid pairing your puppy with a dog who gets too excited or vocal on walks. A puppy is ready to pick up on anything the older dog is feeling, so we want to pair the pup with a calm, easygoing adult dog who will take everything you pass in stride.

2. Most likely, the puppy will try to jump up on the other dog, grab their leash, and generally get in the way. That's normal. Just put more space between the dogs and use treats and your charismatic voice and vibe to redirect pup's interest to you from time to time.

Zigzags and Wiggles Are Okay

The primary goal of the first few weeks of walking is to get the puppy outside the home and feeling great about the world. A puppy in her first months of life is particularly full of curiosity and capacity to learn, and only with leash walks can you make the most of it. There's just not enough new stuff to learn about inside our homes. We want to instill the lesson that novelty is just fine, before biology starts to tell the pup that anything new could be a threat. The only way to do that is to expose the puppy, carefully and always at his comfort level, to new sights, smells, sounds, and situations.

Given that the priority is keeping pup feeling happy, this is not the time for teaching skills like a picture-perfect Heel. It's a time to bring that pouch filled with yummy stuff and teach pup that you, walks, and new things are associated with pleasurable experiences (like food). This is also a time to let pup sniff to his heart's content, because every sniffari helps him learn about the world, which builds confidence.

Don't get frustrated if your walks seem small: they're not small to the pup who has just used her nose to "meet" fifteen dogs, three kids, and an elderly neighbor. There is plenty of time for you to teach your dog to walk steadily ahead with you. Right now, though, as your brand-new puppy learns what the world has to offer, zigzags, wiggles, and sniffs are perfect.

9

CRYING

It's Lonely to Be Somebody's New Puppy

New puppy owners are often shocked by the immediacy, the volume, and the staying power of the cries that penetrate the air when their pup is left alone. While this response may seem over-the-top to humans — "My gosh, I'm just running upstairs to switch the laundry" — it is entirely sensible, and even life preserving, from the puppy's point of view.

Once we understand what's going on in that sweet head, we can begin teaching something new: feeling content while alone.

Why Is Puppy So Sad?

In his life on Planet Dog, your puppy was likely within leaping distance of his mom and all of his brothers and sisters every single second of every day. Is it any wonder that being alone for the first time feels sad and even terrifying? While some pups seem to adjust just fine (you lucky folks can skip this chapter), most need some help feeling safe when they're by themselves.

When you step away, your puppy doesn't know you're just going to get the mail. For all he knows, you have left for good. After all, a few days ago when you picked him up, it turned out he was leaving his littermates forever. I don't mean to make you feel terrible, but truly empathizing with the shocking change your pup has been through is what's going to fuel your patience for this phase in his development.

Create a Positive Association with Alone Time

Our goal is to change how the puppy feels about being alone — from "Uh-oh, I have no idea what this means" to "Hey, I kind of like being by myself."

The first step is to make sure something great happens every time you go away. If it's just for a moment, scatter a little kibble on the floor with a cheery "Find It!" By the time the puppy has found the last bit, you're back. Deliberately repeat this routine over and over throughout the day. (It's fine if your pup gets all of his food in this fashion instead of from a twenty-second gobble from a bowl three times a day.) He's learning it's yummy when somebody leaves the room.

Stockpile a few super-special treats for absences of five to fifteen minutes, such as:

- a LickiMat with peanut butter smeared on it

- a snuffle mat with tiny bits of hot dog throughout — some easy to find and others hidden

- a Toppl (which is easier to excavate than a Kong) filled with a concoction of plain yogurt and kibble

These options are engaging because they immediately smell and taste delicious. You can progress to freezing the LickiMat or the Toppl, which will make them last longer, but in the early stages, that frozen version won't entice your pup because it doesn't have enough of a scent.

Don't use a chew item for this that the puppy could swallow or choke on (see chapter 7), because you won't be supervising. Be very careful, because many things that are marketed for puppies are small enough to make swallowing likely, and many things marketed for chewing can break into sharp pieces.

Use Timing to Encourage Naps

Once your pup has formed a positive association with being alone for short bursts, it's time to stretch that length. Your golden key for this stage is timing. Happily, puppies sleep a lot. Make use of that and give your pup alone time right when she's ready to fall asleep.

For example, if your pup just had a thirty-minute romp with a neighbor pup, a thirty-minute stroll around the block, and some hangout time with your kids, it is a perfect opportunity to experiment with a longer stint alone. Give her a long-lasting treat and head to the next room. Ideally, that chew session will turn quickly into a nap session. Your puppy never has a chance to be sad about being alone because what she needs most is a big sleep.

Many folks have poor results with alone training because they haven't learned the trick of using the puppy's schedule rather than their own to drive this learning. Without considering the nap schedule (and manipulating it, if need be), they put the puppy "away" as soon as their Zoom meeting starts or they need to drive the kids to school, regardless of what the puppy's been up to. If your pup happens to be full of energy and nowhere near ready to nap at that point, then as soon as the special treat is gone, the operatic Song of the Sad Puppy will likely commence.

Here's a special note to those of you (like me) who can barely resist cuddling with a napping puppy: beware. You could be training pup to feel that she can't sleep without that lap. There will be plenty of time after this puppy stage where you can nap with your dog, but for now, a puppy's need for sleep is a wonderful tool that can help us transition her into feeling okay when alone.

Go Back Before She Cries

Let's say your first stab at leaving your puppy to nap worked great, and your exhausted pup fell asleep by herself in the kitchen, just as you planned. It's been an hour, and she's still zonked out! Don't blow it now by heading out for a quick errand. Stay nearby so that you can take the puppy out before she feels lonely. Ideally, when she wakes up, she's aware that she's alone, but it doesn't strike her as a big deal yet because she had a super-nice sleep, and then, before she has time to feel anxious, there you are letting her out. She has just made a positive association with being alone for a long time. It'll make it easier next time. Repeat, repeat, repeat, and you're well on your way to being able to leave her with no problem.

If, instead, you rushed it, went out of earshot, and then came back to a sobbing pup, you have only bad options now. She may have learned that she really is terrified of being alone, or that crying gets her out if she keeps it up long enough, or that nobody will come to her at all, which lessens her feeling of confidence in you. (There are some really sad studies showing what leaving a new human baby to "cry it out" actually teaches them.)

So take a deep breath and understand that you need to go slow to go fast. Be patient these first days and weeks. Giving your pup a chance to warm up to life on Planet Human will pay off enormously as time goes on.

Extra Tip: Masking Noise

You know who the best sleepers often are? The puppies who live in houses with a bunch of young kids. First of all, they're exhausted just by absorbing the activity around them. But second, they get habituated to a constant level of noise, which they learn to ignore.

For other pups, any odd noise can be the nap enemy. Just when your pup was falling asleep, she hears Dad whistling upstairs, or a door slam, or a neighbor dog bark. Suddenly she's jolted into first wondering what that was, and then into realizing that she is alone. Cue the Song of the Sad Puppy.

Background noise can help tremendously. You can put on a sound machine, or classical music, or maybe a YouTube channel with a dull soundtrack. For folks in environments with loud, unpredictable noises (like some apartment buildings), a big box fan can disrupt sound waves in addition to providing masking noise and can truly be a game changer.

For the Pup Who Needs Extra Help

Every now and then there's a pup who, even when you follow these tips at first, has more trouble adjusting to being alone than most.

In that case, follow the same initial steps: tire pup out, wait until it's nap time, hand over a special treat. But then rather than leaving the room, simply sit just out of reach so that Pup can't sit in your lap or curl on your feet. You might sit on the other side of a gate, or right next to her crate. Work on your laptop or read a book, but stay right there as pup enjoys the treat. Don't move around and make the pup think she has to be on guard for your departure. Let her relax into enjoying her treat while you're in sight.

Try that again later in the day. And again later. Now you've created a nice pattern, and she knows what to expect. Patterns are enormously comforting to a worried dog, because they know what's coming next, and they know it's okay. Then build on the pattern as follows:

- Repeat the process, but sit farther away. Is she relaxed and enjoying her treat? Great. Do that a few more times before moving a bit farther away.

- Next, stand up and sit down again while spending time with her. Does she stay relaxed? If so, repeat the process a few more times.

- Try going out of sight for a minute and then coming right back. Success? Repeat a few more times.

- Build duration by leaving the puppy long enough to switch the laundry or get the mail.

A critical part of all alone training is to minimize comings and goings. As you work on this, don't make a big deal of leaving, and don't give a high-energy hello on your return. All that does is confirm to the pup that she's right to feel this is a huge event. Instead, treat it all as no big deal — because it's not.

It's possible that this all strikes you — or your puppy's coparent — as laughable, over-the-top indulgence. You might have heard advice like this:

Just shut him in there and he'll be fine soon enough.
She has to adjust to our life, not the other way around.

The thing is, given what this puppy knows about the new planet he's been taken to — almost nothing — crying for your help is perfectly reasonable. Only you know he's safe. He does not. Let's teach him.

10

THE CRATE

Make It a Happy Place

I know it's hard, but it's worth taking a deep breath and working patiently on happy crating. Once your pup sees her crate as a calm napping spot where she often finds awesome chews, you'll regain a bit of your pre-puppy freedom. A pup who's asleep or occupied in a crate is not peeing on the floor or chewing electrical cords. But our human impatience makes it very common to rush crating, and then to overuse it — both of which may ruin our ability to use the crate at all.

Getting to the point where a puppy views her crate as a safe, relaxing retreat can look very different from pup to pup. Rather than giving you a tangled flowchart of possible steps, I will ask you to simply head back to the previous chapter on alone training. The underlying philosophy is the same. Start with empathy for how unnatural this feels, build positive associations, use a puppy's natural rhythms to set up for success, and don't rush it.

In addition, here are some crate-specific suggestions:

- Get your setup working for you. I keep an open crate (with the favored bed in it) in the Puppy Apartment, so that pup naturally heads in there when she's tired. If you have her comfiest bed right *next* to her crate instead, which spot do you think she'll choose?

- I toss yummy stuff in the crate randomly throughout the day so she learns to explore in there just in case there's something good inside. The more she casually pops in and out of her own accord and forms a positive association with the crate, the better.

- I play around with closing the door while I sit nearby, and I pair that experience with an amazing chew.

Once dogs are past the potty training and heavy chewing stages, I use crates minimally. They're great for when guests first enter, or for when multiple dogs each have their own special chews, or when the plumber is working in the kitchen. Having a dog who's relaxed with the idea of a crate is also helpful when there are medical issues, or when you're staying at somebody else's house. But I've found that when their Planet Dog needs are being met, most dogs can be trusted to handle more space, so crating is needed only occasionally and for short periods.

11

PICKING UP PUPPY

Avoid the Surprise-Swoop-Squeeze

When you see your little puppy, the most natural thing in the world is to run over and swoop her up into your arms for a nice big cuddle.

I beg you: don't do that. It may feel wonderful to you, but you may have just created a moment of fear for that puppy.

Puppies Growl Out of Fear

Style matters, and the seemingly simple pickup approach above includes three unfortunate choices: the surprise, the swoop, and the squeeze. Each of those elements creates discomfort in a being who is new to our human world. (Nobody on Planet Dog picks anybody else up.) To complete the picture of the terror, there's often an additional element: the squeal.

Sometimes people contact me in a panic because the puppy they got last week is growling at them, and it's getting worse every day. A quick home visit usually reveals that these nice folks are in the habit of surprise-swoop-squeeze. They are unintentionally terrifying their pup, and the pup is learning to fend them off with a growl.

While that's a bummer, it's also great news, because it means the owners can probably fix the issue in a jiffy by learning to pick up the puppy in a way that will build the missing trust.

No Surprising

It's scary for puppies to be picked up completely by surprise. One minute they're just hanging out — maybe even sound asleep — and the next they're up in the air. Sure, some pups will roll with it, but for many others it's alarming.

You can avoid the surprise factor by altering your approach. No running. No zooming. Just stroll over so pup has a chance to see you coming. Then crouch down and take a moment to say hi with a gentle stroke. All along, provide a nice, low-volume voice-over for extra reassurance and preparation: "Hi, sweet pup. How about I come say hello?" That advance warning system gives the puppy a chance to catch up to the action.

For a pup who has already been growling about handling, a cue word is a nice thing to add. A consistent heads-up in the form of a cheery "Ready, set, go, time for a pickup!" can be a game changer. It helps pup learn to be ready when that's about to happen and to relax when it's not.

No Swooping

Even if you eliminate the surprise factor, you still may hear a growl if your pup feels unsafe in the air. That's why the second rule of the perfect pickup is this: no swoop-and-dangle allowed. Your new pup doesn't want the thrill of an amusement-park ride.

Help the puppy feel safe with you by picking her up with a slow, cradling motion that keeps her body fully supported: one hand underneath, the other softly against her chest and shoulder. Continue your quiet voice-over: "Aw, there we go, we're just going to move over here, you're my sweetie girl..." Don't stand up too quickly — give pup the old, creaky elevator experience rather than the express ride to the top floor.

If you're doing remedial work, it can help to have a chew, a toy, or a piece of jerky in your hand as you say, "Ready, set, go, time for a pickup!" This way you can distract pup from her worries and create a positive association with the feeling of being handled in this way.

No Squeeze-and-Trap

Once pup is in your arms as you're standing, you can extend his lesson in trust by slowly, gently putting him right back down. For some puppies, the main fear in a pickup is the dreaded squeeze-and-trap. Humans love to trap puppies in what they call a loving hug. The puppy might call it terrifying jail time.

Nobody — not one human, not one animal — wants their body to be held against their will. And yet somehow we think puppies are supposed to sit endlessly in our laps and relish being carried around, so we make them do that regardless of their reaction. Kids are the ones who find this temptation hardest to resist, but I'm amazed at how many adults also refuse to recognize a puppy's squirming as a legitimate plea for bodily autonomy. Pups who are held and carried against their will often grow into dogs who hate being handled. It's sad, because it's the folks who most want cuddly dogs who tend to turn their dogs into resisters.

Here's what I tell kids (and, ahem, a few adults): if you want to be your puppy's favorite, then let that puppy do the choosing, especially at first. Rather than demanding the puppy's attention, entice it instead. Get down on the floor, get a squeaky toy, roll around in a puppy-like way. Soon enough that puppy will start choosing you to play with. And then, miracle of miracles, when he's tired, he'll wander over and choose *your* lap to sleep in. Now you may be just one step away from that pup happily asking to be picked up and cuddled. Yay!

Always Watch Body Language

If you eliminate the surprise-swoop-squeeze from your routine, your pup will soon be calm about being picked up. To see if you're at that point yet, look for the signals that pup is happy about this handling. Is she regularly choosing to approach you? Turning her head toward you instead of away? Relaxing her body against yours?

No longer struggling in your arms? Perfect. Now you can skip the warning cue and the treat in your hand as you lift.

But stick with the no-surprise approach, the soothing voice-over, the unintimidating crouch, and the slow, supported lift. It's habits like those that make people describe you as the one who is "just magic with dogs!"

It's not magic. It's just empathy. Use it, and enjoy the rewards.

Body Handling: First Bath to Vet Visits

In addition to being picked up, puppies will experience a range of body handling throughout their lives. Give your puppy — and yourself — a wonderful gift by gently acclimating her to what's ahead. The more comfortable she is with being handled at home, the more smoothly things will go at the vet or the groomer. (Just think about how scary those experiences might feel!)

People tend to go too big and too fast when it comes to body handling, creating a negative impression that makes everything after that harder. For example, you don't need to give a bath the first day, and you don't have to clip all ten toenails at once. Give yourself, and your pup, a break, and take baby steps.

At first, make a habit of softly touching your puppy's ears and feet — two spots that can be sensitive but often need attention. Start with the lightest amount of pressure for just a moment, and when pup is clearly comfortable, progress to mimicking vet care as you reward. Check puppy's gums while you cheerily talk to her, and then play a fun game of tug. Later, briefly swipe an ear with a tissue, and follow with a bite of cheese.

Body handling will be a part of your pup's life with you. It's worth every extra minute to do it in a way that builds her feeling of safety with you, rather than diminishing it.

PART 3

HOUSEMATES

12

PUPPIES AND LITTLE KIDS

Heaven! (Oh... and Hell)

In the back of our collective mind is a hazy vision where a little boy is meandering through a meadow with his new puppy gazing up at him, the scene softly lit by the fading afternoon sun. We know at a glance that they will grow up together as best friends.

Here is my question: Why doesn't the *other* highlight reel also play as a default in our brains? The one where the parents discover that the kids who are supposed to be over the moon with joy about getting the puppy they'd begged for are:

- constantly crying, "He's biting me!," with the scratched arms to prove it

- sobbing because they were knocked down by the jumping pup for the twentieth time that day

- saying, "I don't like him anymore, give him back," because the puppy tore apart their favorite stuffed animal

I wish *that* vision also came preinstalled, so that I wouldn't have to be the one to break the bad news to exhausted puppy parents: "Well, yeah, for a really long time you'll need to be actively supervising every single moment the kids are with the puppy."

The look in their eyes says it all: they've been had. This is not what they signed up for. Where's the dang meadow?

The good news is that there is plenty you can do to set everybody up for success. Creating the right environment, routine, and habits in those first intense months is worth every bit of effort, because — here's where the meadow's not a lie — few things in life beat the puppy-and-kid-growing-up-together thing.

Get in the Zone

First step: mindset. It's demoralizing to be surprised by difficulties. Instead, take a deep breath and anticipate them. Not only does that let you psychologically gird yourself for a certain level of challenge, but it will result in preparation that means far less of the bad stuff will actually occur.

The adults are not the only ones who need psychological prep. The kids will need reminders to help them be their best selves around the puppy. Practice these sentences:

- She's just a baby.
- We are her teachers.
- She is doing all the things that are normal for puppies to do.
- We need to teach her what humans like to do.
- I know those teeth hurt, but she didn't mean to hurt you.
- Puppies play like that with their very favorite littermates.
- We need to help her find a different way to play with you.

The Critical Importance of Gates and Crates

Having easy ways to separate kids and puppies on a regular basis is the single biggest predictor of household happiness in the puppy-hood months. Puppies and young kids simply cannot hang out together without being managed carefully. Period. I know this is devastating news for parents who were thinking the puppy would be an activity that would keep kids off screens and playing outside while their parents can focus elsewhere.

Not yet. But one day. And to get to that day sooner, you need to do the groundwork by preventing bad habits from getting established. Unsupervised kid-puppy interactions will result in the puppy playing the one super-fun thing she knows: the Puppy Game, the beautiful chase-jump-bite-wrestle game she played endlessly with her littermates. These small people are the closest thing she has to those friends she misses so much. They even squeal like her puppy siblings!

There is a lot to teach young kids about how to act in a way that won't draw out the Puppy Game in the puppy. While that's a work in progress, the key is to have quick separation options at your disposal. Do not hesitate to fill your house with them. Crates, pens, gates, and sofas or benches moved to block critical spots are all your friends. Above all, understand that "free play" with kids and puppies will happen for only a tiny fraction of the day, and it will be completely supervised by you.

Don't panic. It won't always be this way.

No, You Don't Have Enough Chew Toys Yet

Without even seeing your setup, I'm going to tell you this: you don't have enough chew toys, or they're not in the right places. "Huh? My basket is overflowing!" I know. But that's just it, they're over there in the basket, and your kids need to be able to reach them *right now*, because the puppy is about to greet your kindergartner by jumping up and sinking in some teeth.

For people who love to keep the house and yard immaculately tidy all the time, this is challenging news. But your kids must be able to reach out whenever they're going to encounter the puppy and grab a long fluffy fox, a braided felt rope, or a big squishy ball. Over and over and over, they need to be able to teach the puppy that the teeth go on the toy, not on the kid. It may be hard for kids to remember to set themselves up for success this way, which is why you have to help by keeping those toys within easy reach.

Rules for Kids

If you want your adult dog to be safe around kids, teach your kids to treat this impressionable puppy with respect. Set up clear, easy-to-remember guidelines for how to interact with the puppy. Normal kid behavior includes a lot of things that will bring out the worst in a puppy. Save yourself a lot of trouble by having a family meeting (or two, plus a quiz) to discuss these guidelines:

1. **Let the puppy choose whether to interact.** If there were only one rule, it would be this one. The puppy is not a stuffed animal to be grabbed, picked up, trapped in a hug or a lap, moved here and there, or argued over. Show the kids how to entice the puppy instead, using squeaky toys, happy voices, and treats.

2. **Find your slow body.** A running and jumping human creates a running and jumping puppy.

3. **Use your quiet voice.** High-pitched, loud noises get a puppy aroused. Aroused puppies jump, chase, and use their teeth to interact.

4. **Sit on the floor if you want to hold the puppy.** In my house, I insist kids sit criss-cross applesauce on the floor when they hold my foster puppies. If you feel this is draconian, I can tell you stories of dropped puppies with broken legs and dogs who growl at the approach of the children in their household. Kids love to walk around the house holding a puppy, but most puppies hate that.

5. **Let sleeping dogs lie.** Puppies need a lot of sleep, and they should be left alone to get it. This rule can be really difficult to apply when you have a very mouthy or jumpy puppy, because sometimes kids only feel safe approaching the pup when he's sound asleep. Promise me at least that you'll make the kids understand this: if the pup moves away, they should respect that choice *immediately*.

6. **Play fair.** Dangling something in front of a puppy without ever actually giving it to him teaches him not to trust humans and not to play by the rules. That's the opposite of what we want to teach. Use the Golden Rule: play the way you'd want to be played with.

7. **Respect the crate.** It must be the puppy's safe, quiet, private refuge. No climbing in, no teasing.

Find Puppy Playdates

Puppy playdates are wonderful for every puppy household, but particularly critical for homes with young children. If you've ever watched puppies with their littermates, you know that life is one long version of the Puppy Game. Reasonably enough, that's how they expect to interact with humans, too — especially the small, running, squealing kind. It's unfair to spend every day telling our pup "No! Don't bite and wrestle!" Instead, it's on us to find them a friend who'll love to play the Puppy Game.

People new to puppyhood may feel awkward or nervous about asking neighbors for a puppy playdate. But experienced puppy people can tell you that nothing will improve your puppyhood experience faster than finding an awesome puppy friend nearby. Another puppy will match your puppy's over-the-top energy, give him a healthy outlet for his biting and jumping, and build his doggy communication skills, which will keep him safer in encounters with other dogs. (For details on how to supervise that activity, see chapter 21.)

If I could conjure up the perfect family life with a puppy, every day would start with adults enjoying a twenty-minute cup of coffee in a fenced yard with two neighbor puppies playing, and maybe another twenty-minute session with a different furry friend right before the kids come home from school in the afternoon.

If you're lucky, you might have a well-run puppy class nearby that offers some puppy playtime. Just keep an eye on the situation. There are amazing trainers out there who really know how to do this

right, and there are...others. It takes a great setup and skilled oversight to make this a positive experience for all the pups. Watch your
puppy's body language, give your pup a safe little refuge between
your legs or under your chair, and be prepared to bail.

Structure the Togetherness

Free play between kids and puppies often ends in chaos, and that's
not a habit we want them to practice. Having a handful of activities
on tap that give some structure to playtime is key. A few examples:

- A walk is a great option. Heading out on an adventure together can be a perfect way to bond. All parties are interested in the surroundings, so they won't be 100 percent
  focused on each other. Maybe the kids can ride bikes or
  scooters. The pup is on a leash, so it's easy for the kids to
  move out of range if the Puppy Game threatens to start.
  Bring a treat pouch (always), and have the kids reward the
  puppy when she responds to her name with eye contact.

- Playing the Recall game is a twofer: it's fun, *and* it teaches
  the puppy that it pays off to come when called. Just get in a
  circle and take turns calling your pup with a high-pitched,
  cheery "Come, come, come." When puppy spins and runs
  to the person who called, they deliver a treat. Even tiny
  kids can play this game, and it teaches the pup to listen to
  everyone in the family.

- "Find It" can be a surprisingly useful game. Suddenly, a
  puppy is happy to have all four paws on the floor (instead
  of jumping up), and a bitey mouth is pointed toward the
  floor instead of a tender arm. First, the adults need to teach
  the pup that this magic phrase means it's worth looking on
  the ground, because they've just tossed a treat there. Then,
  keep a ceramic jar of kibble where the kids can reach it,
  and teach them to toss a bit of kibble and say, "Find It!"

The pup will snuffle after the treat and then turn back to see what's next. The kid says, "Find It!" again and tosses another treat in a different direction. Repeat, repeat, repeat. As you advance, the pup can learn to Sit to start the next round. (Jumping or mouthing puts a stop to the game.)

• Training is the best game of all when kids are old enough (and have the right temperament) to take part. Positive-reinforcement training should feel like a fun game to the dog, and for the right kid it can be a wonderful thing to do with the puppy. Parents need to be vigilant, though. If your puppy is just learning Sit but you let your second-grader come in and demand Sits in a big voice without offering rewards at the right time, you've just set your training back. (Some kids love telling dogs what to do, so it's key to emphasize that we humans are teachers, not drill sergeants.)

Create a Nap-Filled Routine

Setting up a daily routine for everyone will foster better household interactions. There are going to be times when either a child or a puppy is too wound up (or too tired) to be at their best. Instead of trying to react to those constantly shifting dynamics, you can establish a structure that stacks the deck in your favor.

Building puppy naps into the routine is critical. Often the puppies who are the most jumpy and bitey are the ones who are not getting enough sleep because of their active household. Young puppies should be sleeping at least as much as they're awake during the day for the first few months. In the beginning they may tend to be awake for an hour, then asleep for two hours. Just like toddlers, many puppies think they don't need a nap, so they don't take one by choice. This is where a nice, quiet crate comes in, maybe with a box fan on or classical music playing to mask household noise.

To find the right routine, start with your family schedule, add in the natural rhythms of your puppy, and come up with a daily plan for meals, walks, playdates, indoor training sessions, outdoor Fetch and Tug, and naps. Then adjust as necessary. If your pup is overexcited when your kids first come home from school, experiment with your routine. Does she need a good nap beforehand to be at her best with the kids? Or does a big walk or a twenty-minute romp with the neighbor pup take the edge off her excitement and help her be ready to play without using her teeth?

This kind of careful planning won't be necessary forever, but in the beginning, while you're teaching puppies and kids good habits about how to act around each other, aim to put them together only when they're both at their best.

Puppies and Kids Really Is the Dream

This long list of suggestions might have you throwing up your hands and saying, "Hey! I thought puppies and kids were a natural match!" They absolutely are — when they're set up for success. For a child, there's nothing like growing up with a friend at home who loves you unconditionally; for a puppy, there's nothing like a playful, snuggly kid who has all the time in the world for you. And from a parent's perspective, that relationship is a beautiful thing to witness for years and years, so a few months of this focused management ends up being a drop in the bucket on the way to creating the dream.

13

PUPPIES AND CANINE SIBLINGS

Help Your Adult Dog Like the New Puppy

"Sheesh, I thought my dog would love having a new friend, but he is being so mean to the new little puppy!"

I hear this all the time from shocked owners. But what's surprising to me is not the resident dog's behavior. It is the humans' expectation of immediate bliss.

Sure, this can happen sometimes — particularly if the current dog is very young and lives for playdates with his neighborhood friends. Then the arrival of a puppy really is a "You had me at hello" moment worthy of TikTok.

But that instant-friends scenario is not the norm. To understand why, think about how *you* would feel if your parents decided that you needed a new best friend — and then:

- They brought a stranger home to live with you, 24/7.

- It turns out their idea of a great friend for you is a toddler. What the heck? This isn't play, it's babysitting. It's exhausting and boring at the same time.

- You're apparently supposed to allow the weird toddler to climb all over you until you're bruised, and to let him take your stuff and chew on it until it's ruined.

- To make things worse, your parents are so absorbed with the new kid that the best parts of your daily life have now disappeared.

- The final straw: when you accept the babysitting situation

71

and try to teach the toddler good manners, your parents are mad at you all the time, saying, "Don't be so mean!"

See? We should not be amazed when a dog is not thrilled with the new puppy.

Smoothing the Way

Typically, on day 1, resident dogs are anywhere from a little unsure to definitely not in favor. Don't worry. There will likely be incremental progress every day, or even a dramatic turnaround in seventy-two hours. While there will be some sad cases where an adult dog cannot accept a puppy even when you're doing everything right, in the vast majority of cases, by the third week things have settled down nicely.

This is not to say that I agree with the advice, commonly given to folks whose older dog is not enjoying the puppy, to "just let them work it out." When there are half a dozen easy things we can do to smooth the beginning of that friendship, why would we subject two beloved dogs to the fear, sadness, and frustration involved in working it out themselves?

Here's how you can ease the transition for your older dog, create a safer and more developmentally positive scenario for your puppy, and increase the odds that the two will quickly become real friends.

Puppy Contact Is Always Optional

An older dog should never, ever be forced to hang out with a puppy. Use gates, crates, benches, and whatever else you have to create a situation where your older dog can always escape and head to a peaceful "adult swim" scenario elsewhere in the house.

Puppies can be rude. For your dog, spending time with a puppy is not the same as playing with a fun adult dog. While some dogs are incredibly tolerant of all of the mouthing and jumping — and even seem to relish the babysitting job — others are understandably horrified at first. If you trap your adult dog with the puppy, you are asking too much. Your dog will be stressed and sad, and your puppy may end up hurt.

Keep in mind that the no-forcing advice goes both ways: super-friendly adult dogs can be overwhelming to new puppies. Make sure a little puppy has a few easy retreats — perhaps under couches and chairs — so that she also has a chance to opt in or out of interaction depending on comfort level. Let them both choose all of this at their own pace (which may not be your preferred pace).

Let Your Adult Dog Growl

It's not unusual for an older dog to give small warning growls or snaps while interacting with a new puppy. I cringe when I hear people scolding the dog: "Shadow, be nice!" Shadow *is* being nice, by agreeing to hang out with this toddler at all. The least you can do is let Shadow use the tools at his disposal to teach the puppy important lessons.

The fastest way to convince an older dog that this puppy really is an awful turn of events is to pair the puppy's presence with the feeling that the adult dog is constantly on the verge of being in trouble: "Whenever I interact with that puppy, Mom is mad at me."

If you have ill-advisedly trapped your older dog with the puppy, then the resulting growls and snaps could in fact be dangerous. However, if you have made interacting optional, then you know that Shadow has actually *chosen* to be with the puppy. In that case, his growl, and that scary-looking little snap/snarl, are part of healthy boundary setting. Shadow's efforts to teach good dog manners — worrisome as it may look to you — will help the puppy interact more safely with other dogs in the long run.

So here's what to say instead of that threatening "Be niiice" when you hear a growl. Try "Good job, Shadow! Thank you." And mean it. When your adult dog feels your support, he's going to be even more solid in his interactions with this pup.

Don't Change Your Dog's Best Stuff

When people adopt a new puppy (or for that matter, welcome a new baby into the home), they know there's going to be total disruption for a short time. But they are sure that eventually normalcy will return.

You know who *doesn't* know that? The resident dog. So the very kindest thing you can do is to identify the three most important things in your dog's life and make sure they are undisturbed by the arrival of the interloper. Maybe the morning walk with Dad? The after-work game of Fetch with Mom? The daily playdate with Rover across the street? Whatever your dog loves best, leave those cornerstones of a happy life in place when the puppy shows up. If the puppy's arrival is paired with the loss of Shadow's very favorite things, how do you think he'll feel about the puppy? Giving your dog stability will help him be at his generous best with the new puppy.

Exhaust Your Puppy Elsewhere

Most of the time, the new puppy's favorite thing will be the resident dog. As flattering as that may look, it is hard to be on the receiving end of that much enthusiastic physical affection all day long.

Do your dog a favor and find some other friends for your puppy to adore. Ideally, there is another puppy right up the street, and a few times a week you can take all those sharp teeth and the wild jumping and pair your pup with a like-minded buddy. Perhaps you can make use of a great rewards-based puppy kindergarten class nearby, complete with well-supervised puppy socials. You know what happens next? You get to bring home a very chill puppy, who might suddenly strike your older dog as kind of a nice kid.

Two Dogs Means *Duck! Feta! Fish!*

Finally, start to create some fun new experiences for your older dog that happen only when the puppy is around. Find a treat that you've never given to your dog before. Maybe it's those dried fish bits at the pet store or the feta cheese in your fridge. Whatever it is, bring it out a few times a day and give it to both dogs only when they're together. Voilà! Even if your dog isn't yet actually enjoying the company of the puppy, at least you're giving him a reason to want to be near the toddler every now and then.

Most of the time, two dogs really are more fun than one. Folks who've lived amid a true doggy friendship witness so much shared joy that it's hard for them to imagine having only one dog at a time. The thing is, we humans have a tendency to jump ahead. We get that puppy and immediately envision the happy ending, forgetting to focus on how to get there. As a result, our trusted old friend and our brand-new one have to go through a rocky phase. The whole household is stressed.

It doesn't have to be that way. Just a little empathy combined with a solid initial plan can create a calm on-ramp to what may well be that dream friendship.

14

PUPPIES AND CATS

Create a Peaceable Kingdom

According to family lore, when my husband was a little boy, his bedtime request was always the same: "Tell me a story about a doggy and a kitty who made friends." Those of us who have navigated the doggy-kitty waters know that he was onto something. This scenario has drama, surprise, even a bit of danger — all with the potential for a blissfully happy ending. Luckily, in real life, you can skip much of the suspense and get straight to the good part.

The First Minute Matters

If you take away only one message from this chapter, make it this: *you don't get a second chance at the first minute.*

The time to think about facilitating a good canine-feline introduction is way before you bring the new pet home. You're going to have a lot on your mind on that day. The first moments in the house together can set the tone for this new dynamic. If you've taken a spontaneous "Oh, they'll work it out" approach and the predictable chase ensues, you have already blown it.

That drama is easy to prevent with just a little planning. The most frustrating call I get is the one that begins: "Oh, I meant to have the dog in the crate when we came in with the new kitty, but we were so excited we just forgot. There was a chase. Honestly, Rover just wanted to play! He didn't mean any harm. But, um, Fluffy hasn't come out from under the bed for two days. What do we do now?"

Unfortunately, you can't turn back the clock and get that all-important first hour back.

Wait on the Intro

The new pet has a lot to take in at first: new people, new home, new vibe. Make the transition easier by postponing the much-anticipated dog-cat introduction until the newcomer has had time to settle in. For example, if you're adding a kitty to the home, you may want to keep her in a bedroom for anywhere from an afternoon to a few days as you bond with her.

Allowing the puppy and the cat to sniff each other under a bedroom door before they see one another can be a perfect start. Without the intensity of visual stimulus, the interaction is often calmer. You can exchange some of their bedding materials to allow closer investigation of those new smells.

Once the new kid is a bit settled, it's time for a formal introduction. Ideally, you'll get a ho-rum reaction along the lines of "Oh, it's the dude from under the door."

Contain the Doggy

There are two keys to the best introductions: canine containment and feline confidence. Think hard about how you can reinforce both.

Typically, a dog is the more excited part of the new duo, which is why that's the one you'll want to contain. This is true even for a little, seemingly harmless puppy. People often discount the emotional trauma an exuberant puppy can cause. If you want a dog and a cat to become friends, you'll start by keeping Rover from getting in Fluffy's space.

If Rover is comfortable with a crate, that's the ideal place for him when he's first meeting Fluffy. Alternatively, you can use gates or pens to establish a safe separation. Either option has the advantage of leaving your hands free and letting you move between the pets to manage the situation and deliver treats.

While keeping a puppy on leash for the intro can work, it's less optimal because:

- your hands are occupied with the leash, so it's harder to dispense treats and petting.

- you're going to get tired of holding on — which could lead to a slipup.

- if you are letting your leashed dog pull you around after the kitty, the kitty will feel she can't escape from the dog, so her anxiety will go through the roof.

Tethering the leash to a securely fixed object can mitigate some of these issues, but crates and gates will likely result in a better experience for the initial phase.

Give the Kitty a High Retreat

With the exception of the very young and the very old, most cats can jump and climb up to spots a puppy can't reach. The faster Fluffy figures that out, the faster you're on your way to a peaceful home. A high, safe perch gives the kitty that all-important confidence that she's got some control over the situation, which will allow her to entertain the idea of exploring a friendship.

Before the big day, ponder the possible cat perches in your house. The size and agility of the dog will determine whether that will be a chair, a table, a counter, or the top of the refrigerator. You may need to do a little rearranging to make sure it's easy for Fluffy to reach, not too cluttered for her to use, and impossible for Rover to get to. Help Fluffy learn that this is her spot by putting a bed there and bringing her there often for treats and petting. (Fluffy can eventually learn that many tall spots offer retreats, but we want her to know she has at least one safe place.)

If it's in your budget and you can get over the effect it has on your decor, get a giant kitty condo or tree. The carpet covering offers a secure grip for a scared cat climbing to safety. The most fun ones have landings at different heights, so that as Fluffy gains confidence, she can choose to hang out just a bit closer to Rover.

I bought a monstrosity from Chewy.com that I adore. (Goodbye, nice dining room.) It's brought me peace of mind because Mr. Bojangles knows he can streak up his tall treehouse if a new foster dog chases him. And feeding him up there is a great way to keep the dogs out of the cat food.

Learn Body Language

Now that you've figured out how you'll contain the puppy, and where you'll encourage your cat to stay out of reach, it's time to introduce the two. Sometimes, that moment will be such a nonevent that you'll feel off-duty almost immediately. More likely, though, you'll be spending hours, days, or even weeks watching your pets' body language and being ready to intervene.

Familiarize yourself with warning signs:

- If Rover is stiffening and staring, take a break.

- If Fluffy's ears are pinned back and her tail is swishing back and forth, take a break. (Remember that the cat can be the one to do harm!)

Reward Calm

While you want to be ready to take quick action if the dog-cat session gets intense, you also want to reward calm behavior. Have amazing treats within reach. If possible, have a second person available so that each pet has a handler.

Perhaps Rover's in a crate with you sitting next to him as another family member calmly brings Fluffy to her now-familiar spot on top of her kitty condo. Or Fluffy is in her newly claimed spot on the kitchen counter, and someone brings Rover to the gate just outside the kitchen.

The moment Fluffy is in sight, offer Rover bites of hot dog, feta cheese, ham, or whatever is new and exciting to him. This is a three-pronged strategy:

- It distracts him from the kitty.

- It rewards him for doing something other than obsessively focusing on the kitty.

- It helps him build a positive association with the kitty. "Oh! So the presence of this cat means I get amazing treats I've never had before! Huh. I like this cat."

Use tiny, pea-sized treats so you can keep up a stream of food delivery. If he's too excited to take them, increase his distance from the kitty. When he's eating them calmly, you can begin offering cues, if he knows any yet — Sit, Down, Spin, Touch — to help take his mind off the kitty.

As for Fluffy, have one person standing nearby, offering a sense of security, with petting and treats. If Fluffy realizes the dog can be in sight without being a threat, she may well go into "boring kitty" mode, which is ideal. The last thing we want is a cat who darts so very provocatively — which is why you want to do everything you can to calm Fluffy (without restraining her, which would set progress way back).

It may be that five minutes is plenty for the first introduction. Help both pets go back to their separate areas of the home, and then repeat the process every few hours. Soon enough, both will anticipate what's next. Ideally, Rover will run over, and rather than thinking, "Ooh, a kitty to chase," he's thinking, "Ooh, time for me to Sit for a hot dog." As Fluffy sees Rover approach her perch, rather than thinking, "Oh no!," she's thinking, "This is where he sits, he doesn't bother me, and I get those crunchy treats I never get any other time."

Make no mistake: these early sessions are a lot of work for the humans. The process is fascinating, though, and in the end it can pay off dramatically, with a smooth and relatively quick path to calm. As you witness both parties relaxing, it's time to slow the stream of treats and let them begin to focus on each other from time to time without trying to distract them.

If you're lucky, Fluffy may decide that it might be fun to reach down and experiment. You'll know things are going well when the kitty starts to dangle a tail, or a paw. You're on your way to the two of them figuring out how they can play together.

Enjoy the Unfolding Story

Two decades ago, we had two dogs and a desire for a cat. On the face of it, it looked a bit ill-advised, since Shadow was a strong, athletic wolf hybrid (don't ask) whose intensity around small running things indicated this could be dicey. On the plus side, though:

- Our dogs were well trained.

- We knew Piper, our little yellow Lab, would be best friends with the kitty in no time.

- I was wildly interested in this prospect from all angles, and I was the one who would be home all the time to do the work.

We headed to the animal shelter with our kids and asked those smart folks which of the thirty or so cats there might be a good choice for us. They pointed out two, we chose one, and headed home to start a months-long journey of gates and leashes and treats.

At first Shadow was a shaking, drooling mess any time he was near the kitty. But Fritzy just looked at him calmly — truly almost rolling his eyes — waiting for him to become civilized.

At some point the novelty wore off just enough, the treats smelled just delicious enough, and Shadow's pack instinct ("Oh, we're family") kicked in just enough. His body language no longer worried me. Still, I wasn't about to remove our gates. But then Fritzy leapt over them. Once my heart came back down from my throat, I realized we'd done it.

Soon they were the classic "doggy and kitty who made friends," curled up together on the bed, much to my husband's delight.

15

PUPPIES AND SPOUSES

Get on the Same Page

When I get an email asking for help with a six-month-old puppy who's still not house-trained, I'm ready to bet that person doesn't live alone. There's probably a spouse, or maybe some teenagers.

How do I know? Because in a single-person scenario, the person who wanted the dog in the first place is both setting and following the rules. With messaging that is 100 percent consistent, a puppy learns quickly.

In contrast, as wonderful as a "village" of loved ones can be for a puppy, it usually slows training. That may sound counterintuitive — shouldn't more helping hands make things easier? — but the more humans in the household, the higher the chance that they are sending the puppy mixed messages.

Potty Training

Because of the relentless nature of early potty training, that's where problems first show up. Sure, maybe everyone's on board for the first few days. But then, inevitably, the teenager is in the middle of a potentially high-scoring game, or the husband is on a Zoom call, and the killer thought comes up: "Oh, whatever. Who in the world could keep up this outside-every-thirty-minutes thing? I'll just clean it up later, and nobody will know."

Ack! The bright line has been crossed. When even one member of the household gives up on getting the pup out in time, puppy learns that relieving herself inside offers an immediate reward — "Aah! That feels better!" That's the definition of how to strengthen a behavior. Days, weeks and even months later, the committed member of the household is mystified by why potty training is taking so long.

Household frustration starts to build. Ideally, it is not directed at the puppy, who is simply learning what she's taught.

Jumping Up

Teaching a puppy not to jump up takes tremendous consistency. The humans must actively anticipate that moment, and dramatically reward a different behavior, like playing Find It, sitting, or using a tug toy for greetings. It's a ton of work, over and over again, all day.

That's why it is infuriating when one household member comes home after a long day away and reverses all that learning. The door's flung open, and a glorious full-body, paws-on greeting ensues. The puppy is thrilled to learn that jumping is just like the lottery — you have to play to win!

Once again, household frustration starts to build. Ideally, it is not directed at the puppy, who is simply learning what he's taught.

The Forbidden Couch

Let's say that in the quest to get a "Yes, we can get a puppy" response from a reluctant spouse, the aspiring dog lover has made promises. "Of course puppy won't be allowed on the couch!"

Months later, though, while the reluctant spouse is out of the house, the dog lover figures what they don't know won't hurt them and encourages the dog to cuddle on the couch. Another bright line has been crossed. The snuggling feels so nice for both human and puppy that it happens again and again. Two weeks later, the reluctant spouse is shocked when their dog confidently leaps onto the couch to settle in.

Yet again, household frustration starts to build. Ideally, it is not directed at the puppy, who is simply learning what she's taught.

Talk It Out

I've highlighted three common areas of challenge here, but the list could go on and on. No matter what you're trying to teach your puppy, if somebody in his life is teaching him the opposite, there's going to be trouble.

The solution starts with talking it out. Here are the two key ideas to get across:

1. "Think how hard this is on our dog!" Often a family member believes they're giving the dog a happy time by letting the rules slide on occasion. In truth, they're setting the dog up for confusion and stress. One of the kindest things you can do for your dog is to make Planet Human more consistent and predictable.

2. "You matter! You play a key role." People who let the rules slide usually don't grasp just how much their approach is slowing the puppy's training. In the back of their minds, they've simply been assuming that one day he'll naturally be potty trained or grow out of jumping. Nope! That will not happen. Whenever you're around the puppy, you're teaching something, whether you intend to or not.

Look for Compromise

That simple discussion may well lead to everyone getting on board. But it also may reveal something more difficult: a lack of consensus on the right way to live with the dog. The truth is, we don't all agree on this. It is 100 percent fine if you and I see things differently — unless we live under the same roof with the same dog.

I got an email the other day from a woman who was about to move in with her boyfriend, whose dog, she says, "needs training." She wanted me to work with the dog, listing a dozen behaviors she doesn't want to live with. Hmm. Since the boyfriend was not cc'd on the email, nor was he to be a part of this training session, I suspect he is just fine with the way he's living with his dog. There is trouble ahead there.

The first order of business is to accept that there is no universal list of mandatory dog behaviors decreed from on high. It may seem obvious to one of you that your dog shouldn't sleep in bed with you — and just as obvious to the other that that's the whole point of having a dog. Because it's imperative that there is clear direction for the dog, it's time for an official household meeting about what you each want life with a dog to look like. When there's disagreement, dig deeper, because as you talk out the whys of each of your desires, solutions can arise.

Let's take the case of a husband welcoming the dog jumping up on him in greeting, while the wife is trying to keep the dog from jumping on everybody else. That issue can have a surprisingly simple solution: put the jumping up on cue. We do that at our house because we are weirdly fond of our giant dog's exuberant hello. Whenever we come home, we enter saying, "Wait." Once we've put down our groceries or whatever, we tap our shoulders and say, "Big hug!" George, our ninety-pound adolescent, happily complies. The dog gets 100 percent consistent direction, and we get to enjoy his jumping up when we want it, and not when we (or others) don't.

With just a little thought, it's surprising how many disagreements over dog behavior can result in a solid compromise plan that works for everyone.

•   If one person wants to feed the dog table scraps and other family members don't want a dog staring at them all through dinner, what if you wait until you clear the table, and dish out that food by the sink?

•   If one person wants to snuggle with the dog on movie night, and someone else doesn't want dog fur all over the couch, what if you make sitting on the couch by invitation only? Ask the dog to stay in a Sit on the floor, then put the special blanket on the key couch spot, and say, "Couch time!"

- If one person loves to sleep with the dog but the partner doesn't want to feel squished in bed, how about if the early-to-bed person enjoys dog cuddles until the partner goes to bed? Or what if the dog jumps in for that last hour in the morning once the early riser is gone? I have many clients who do this, and their dogs completely understand the drill.

Long ago, dog training advice was cut-and-dried. Trainers proclaimed one set of rules, as if every dog and owner were the same. But of course that's ridiculous. Gather your household and decide what you want, then commit to teaching it. When the message is consistent and clear from everyone in the house, your dog can learn incredibly nuanced things.

PART 4

SOCIALIZATION

16

THE PUPPY SHOT DILEMMA

Get Out There, but Be Smart

There's a stretch in puppyhood — through the age of four months — when puppies have started their distemper-parvovirus vaccination series but cannot be considered fully immunized.

A convincing swath of research has identified that exact same stretch of time as the almost magical period when pups are uniquely open to new experiences that can set them up for a lifetime of confidence.

The tension between those two scientific truths presents puppy owners with a dilemma after bringing home an eight-week-old pup. Staying at home during those first months is the only way to keep a pup 100 percent safe from infectious disease, but the lack of socialization could lead to debilitating behavioral issues down the road.

So what's an owner to do?

Combining Safety and Socialization

The safest all-around approach is to thread the needle: provide socialization experiences while continually assessing disease risks and making educated choices.

Historically, veterinarians advised owners to keep their pups at home until they were fully immunized. (Simply keeping a distance from other dogs isn't enough, because disease can lurk in the environment.) In recent decades, however, we have learned how harmful it is for a pup to miss out on socialization during this unique developmental stage. In fact, according to a 2018 statement from the American Veterinary Society of Animal Behavior (AVSAB, veterinarians who are board-certified in behavior): "The primary and most important time for puppy socialization is the first three months of life. During this time puppies should be exposed to as many new people, animals, stimuli and environments as can be achieved safely....It should be the standard of care for puppies to receive such socialization before they are fully vaccinated."

All of those interactions — provided they truly feel positive — will help puppies to confidently approach new things for the rest of their lives. Since you can't plan to introduce a dog to every single thing he'll ever encounter, the goal is to help a dog feel comfortable with novelty itself. The benefits that follow cannot be overstated: a higher likelihood of happy walks amid other dogs and people, easy hosting of friends, stress-free gatherings with extended family, calmer vet visits, and the delight of taking your friendly dog on vacation.

While some vets still advise waiting — after all, it's much easier guidance for clients to follow — most now advise careful socialization. (Note that the risks of parvo and distemper vary by region, so vet advice will vary as well.)

The Danger of the Cocoon

Experienced trainers will not only suggest but will plead with owners to get the puppy out and about. The consequences of a puppy's isolation during that key developmental stage can be heartbreaking.

If you wait to venture out of the home cocoon until all shots are complete, you've put yourself on a difficult road. Starting at around four months of age, biology tells a puppy that anything new and different might be a threat. If you don't do the work to combat that message, you may end up with a dog who is anxious around new people, other dogs, or unfamiliar places. Until you live with a dog like that, you can't understand just how sad and difficult it is.

Is it possible to make progress on feeling comfortable in the world after the prime socialization window closes? Absolutely. But it is much harder and more time-consuming.

I foster litters of puppies, safely exposing them to everything that I can in their time with me. I've seen firsthand what happens when, after adoption, socialization comes to an abrupt halt, and the pup spends the next two months "safe" in her own predictable house. At the six-month mark, the well-intentioned owners are devastated about their now-fearful pup, explaining, "It struck us that two months wasn't very long to wait, and we thought we could just make up for it later." Alas, that's not the case. So get your pup out into the world, but be smart about it.

Make Nuanced Choices

The first rule is easy: avoid unknown dogs and the places they frequent, because you don't know whether those dogs are vaccinated or might be sick. Don't take your pup to dog parks, pet stores, or animal shelters until he's fully protected by that last vaccination.

Everything else falls into the "well, it depends" category. Start with your inner circle. If your family and friends all vaccinate their dogs, great! Their houses are safe, so go visit. If your neighborhood is filled with responsible folks who vaccinate their dogs, great! Go ahead and walk your puppy around the block, and stop off to say hi at different houses.

Beyond the inner circle, everyone has to make their own decisions about risk. I personally opt for more exposure to the world. Parvo and distemper are rare in my area, vaccination rates are high, people tend to pick up dog poop, and I avoid walking with puppies in grassy areas where dogs might have pooped previously. I take puppies on the sidewalks and even to the stores at local strip malls to get them comfortable with all sorts of things they don't encounter at home: strangers in hats, kids running, people using wheelchairs, trucks backing up, automatic doors, tile floors. That setting is gold if you keep it right at your pup's comfort level.

Even in an environment you're uncertain about — like a city park — you can protect your pup by putting a blanket on the ground for her to sit on as you sip coffee on a bench. Lots of people use strollers to get their pups used to the sights, sounds, and smells of the big city while keeping their paws safely off the ground. (You can even wash your puppy's paws afterward at home for an extra level of protection.)

Reducing Health Risks in Puppy Playdates

Puppy playdates deserve a special mention here. I highly encourage these (see chapter 21), but of course, like your own pup, the youngest friends are not yet fully vaccinated. That's okay, but it means you need to be careful. Play only with pups who:

- have been in their homes for at least two weeks (something contagious contracted at the breeder or shelter would show up by then)
- are exhibiting absolutely no symptoms
- are in the middle of their vaccination series with a vet
- belong to an owner who is being careful about disease exposure

You may be able to find a well-run puppy class that offers just this scenario.

Remember that you can stack the deck in your pup's favor in other ways, too. In addition to staying right on track with vaccinations, you can help your puppy develop a healthy immune system with good nutrition, regular deworming, parasite preventatives, and good hygiene.

Now, get that puppy out where careful exposure to the wider world can help her become a behaviorally sound adult.

17

PEOPLE, PLACES, AND THINGS

Teach That "New" Is Not Scary

Puppy socialization just might be the most important thing you'll ever do for your dog. As outlined in the previous chapter, the first four months of a puppy's life hold special potential to determine his confidence as an adult. Pups who have a range of positive experiences with the wider world in that time frame are much less likely to become skittish or fearful adult dogs.

Sounds like a great opportunity, right? Except it also sounds like a lot of pressure on owners. Unfortunately, awareness of that ticking clock (only fourteen weeks!) can push people into going overboard in introducing their pup to new experiences, which has the tragic effect of accomplishing the exact opposite of the goal. Why? Because that sensitive period works both ways.

Let's say two owners want to be sure their puppy turns out to be great with kids, and they know these early weeks are key. One takes their pup on a well-intentioned trip to the soccer game sidelines, where he is suddenly swarmed by squealing kids who grab him and pass him around. The other arranges a carefully supervised visit from the three nicest neighbor children, who sit on the floor dangling fun toys and hoping the pup will choose their lap.

These two experiences might not look too different to an inexperienced owner. (They wouldn't have to me, thirty years ago with my first puppy.) But later on, the soccer-game puppy may need to be crated whenever kids are around because he's so nervous, and the neighbor-kids puppy may waggily insist on being included in every chaotic birthday party.

To get socialization right, owners have to walk a tightrope. They need to gently expose the puppy to all sorts of new sights, sounds, smells, people, places, and surfaces — all without letting the puppy feel scared. (A momentary startle is okay, but the pup should bounce back quickly.) It takes education and planning to make the most of this short phase, but the payoff is huge.

What follows is a guide to general socialization (see the next chapter for specifics on dog-to-dog socialization). If you have a pup who seems to easily roll with everything under the sun, this entire approach may strike you as overkill. For sure, some pups are way more confident than others, for reasons we may never fully understand: genes, early learning, environment, karma? But you'll never know where your pup is on that spectrum unless you make a point of watching how she reacts to a wide variety of new experiences. Trainers see the consequences when an owner has missed the fact that their pup needed more exposure. Those owners would urge you to err on the side of overkill. They wish they had.

If your pup continues to happily, eagerly investigate each new thing you put in front of her, this process will all be quick and easy for you. But if she ever turns out to be a bit hesitant, these detailed instructions will help you turn things around.

Earn Your Puppy's Trust

The first step in socializing a puppy is to build trust. Studies show that the youngest puppies can happily handle new things as long as the mama dog is right there. Take away the mom, though, and suddenly that loud noise feels scary. Once you bring a puppy home, *you* have the chance to become the security blanket that helps your puppy to bravely explore the world.

To succeed at that, be a calm, consistent, gentle, positive presence at home. The puppy needs to learn to feel totally safe with you. (Try not to mess up and yell when you see a puddle on the floor.) The more a puppy trusts you, the more easily he'll gain the confidence to explore new situations with you by his side.

Learn Body Language

Before you start introducing potentially startling elements of Planet Human to this toddler from Planet Dog, learn about your puppy's body language. Puppies can't say the words "I'm scared," but their bodies are constantly talking to those who will listen.

Most owners will pick up on the puppy equivalent of screaming: trembling, pulling away, hiding. But there are many more-subtle ways that a dog can reveal discomfort, and they can be easily missed. (See chapter 19.)

Give the Puppy a Choice

While you're refining your observational skills, there's an easy trick that lets you off the hook: simply give the puppy space, and let him choose whether and at what pace to proceed.

- **Let him walk.** You'll learn a lot about how a puppy's feeling about something based on whether he walks toward it or away from it. That's why it's better, if you can, to put pup on the ground in new situations. Watch the choices he makes.

- **Don't pull the leash.** Dragging him toward something new will not make him "get used to it." Instead it may well make him scared of it (and less trusting of you) forever.

- **Never trap the puppy.** Feeling trapped — by a leash, by a hug, by a circling crowd, by a tiny hallway — makes any new experience scary. Always provide an easy escape.

By giving your pup agency like this throughout a new experience, you'll increase the odds that it will imprint positively on him and make him a more confident adult.

Make Experiences Positive

The goal of socialization is to help your puppy form positive associations with all sorts of novel experiences. We could never

introduce a pup to everything he'll encounter later in life, so instead
we teach a puppy to feel great about novelty itself. We want the
adult dog to see something he hasn't seen before and think, "Huh. I
don't know what that is, but there's no reason to worry."

To accomplish that, exposure alone is not enough. Here's how
to stack the deck so that things feel positive:

1. **Use a happy voice.** As your pup's guide to Planet Human,
   you want to set the tone. Use a calm demeanor and a happy
   voice as you narrate what's happening. "Hey! I see a bike!
   Do you see that bike? It's okay, it's just a bike." (Oh, you
   feel silly talking to your dog so much in public? I'm over it,
   and happy to provide that entertainment to strangers. For
   more on why it's so important to narrate your dog's world,
   see chapter 20.)

2. **Never force.** Is pup hesitating? That's okay. Be patient. If
   pup needs more distance, give it by cheerily moving in a
   different direction: "Hey, that's a truck! Let's head over here
   so we can watch it from a distance."

3. **Use food.** Get out that treat pouch! Delicious food is the
   easiest, most direct way to form a happy link between an
   experience and a pup. If your pup pulls back at a giant flag
   waving, respond with, "Oh, look, it's a flag! Here's some
   chicken!" Pup will start to like flags.

4. **Don't lure.** Resist the temptation to lure the pup by plac-
   ing a treat just out of reach in the direction of a scary thing.
   You don't want to poison the power of food by linking it
   with a feeling of fear. Instead, as he makes his own choice
   to look at or move toward the new thing, you can follow up
   with a bite of cheese. It's a small but important distinction.

5. **Know when to quit.** If you had a plan to have the puppy
   meet the plumber who's working downstairs, but you've
   walked into the room with a happy vibe, sat with pup at
   a distance, given a salmon treat every time he looks at the

guy, and pup still wants to head for the hills, call it quits for today. Go play with a squeaky toy upstairs.

Start at Home

Now that you understand how to introduce the pup to the world in a nuanced manner, it's time to get started. Great socialization begins at home, where the puppy is most confident. There is no generic must-do list of people, places, and things — since our goal is demystifying "novelty" in general — but I include examples below for inspiration. Even the tiniest of apartments can be an adventureland for a little puppy if you just put on your thinking cap. Put a blank sheet of paper on the fridge and record one new thing you do each day.

Remember, you're using the tips above to guide every new experience. Here's what that looks like for the first example on the list — wearing different hats. While the puppy is relaxed and looking at you, show her a hat and give her a treat. Let her investigate the hat, and give her another treat. Continue at her pace until she's absolutely relaxed around the hat, then put it on, and immediately take it off. Toss her a treat. If she's unfazed, do it again. Toss another treat. Continue until the puppy is eagerly awaiting you putting on the hat because it means another treat is coming her way. Next, keep the hat on and do some fun training, as long as the pup is engaged with you and not worried. The next day, try a different hat. All okay? Then, instead of letting the pup see you putting on the hat, try just walking into the room with the hat on. Take it off immediately as you say, "It's okay, that's just my hat!" At any point, if the pup is worried for more than a few seconds, call it a day. Start again the next day at a lower intensity.

Mimic this stair-step approach for each of the other items on this list, or any others you might add. Mind you, some dogs will be so obviously confident about some of these new experiences that you'll be able to go from introduction to high-intensity interaction almost immediately. Progress with others may feel excruciatingly slow, but keep it up, because it works.

- Play music.

- Walk around with a backpack on.

- Click across the floor in heels, and walk in clunky boots.

- Do some sizzling, aromatic cooking.

- Starting with the pup in the next room, run the blender, the vacuum, or the hair dryer for just a few seconds. Does pup come to investigate? Great.

- Move a chair or a side table to the middle of the room. (Don't skip this one! So easy.)

- Drape a sheet between two kitchen chairs, letting it dangle.

- Take "field trips" to parts of the house the pup doesn't usually see. Play there for a few minutes.

- Carry a big box.

- Drop a book.

- Put on TV shows that have sounds the puppy otherwise won't hear, such as kid voices, screeching tires, sirens, or laugh tracks.

- Put a crinkly tarp or aluminum foil on the floor for a bit, so pup can investigate and, ideally, walk across it.

- If you have a battery-operated holiday decoration or kid toy that moves or sings, put it at the far end of the room and let puppy investigate it.

- Invite over one nice, calm neighbor who will respect the instruction to wait for puppy to choose whether to interact. If that goes well, progress to more people, more movement, and more volume over time. (The standard recommendation to introduce one hundred people in the first one hundred days is a helpful principle, but it can be interpreted in such a way that owners provide quantity exposure over quality exposure, which backfires.)

- Sit on your front stoop when pup might get to see bikes, strollers, and skateboards go by — all from the safety of his home.

- Since you know when the garbage truck will come by, use that info. Take puppy to watch from the window and be ready with treats. "Yay! It's a truck!"

Big families with young kids will not have to work quite as hard at introducing novelty, because there is always something happening that is new, loud, and filled with motion. It's empty nesters like me, and folks who live alone, who need to work a little harder to vary our routines.

Field Trips

Of course there's only so much your puppy can learn about the world from the confines of your own home, and that's why it's critical to get out and about. Wait a week or two after the pup's arrival to make sure she has transitioned comfortably to your household and views you as her rock, and then plan some outings.

That planning element is key for two reasons. The first is the puppy's health. (See the previous chapter for tips on how to plan safe outings for a pup who isn't yet finished with the distemper-parvo vaccination series.) The second reason is that you need to be 100 percent attentive to your pup if socialization is to be effective. It might seem like a great idea to bring the puppy along on all your errands. Nope! Don't try to multitask. If there's a sale at the dog-friendly garden store, go spend a lovely hour selecting your plants — and leave puppy home at nap time with a Toppl. Go back there the next day for an adventure with your puppy, when you can focus 100 percent on his body language and adjust your plan based on his needs. Maybe you're thinking you don't have time for separate trips, but this puppy activity can be a big success at the five-minute mark.

Here are some ideas for outings:

- Visit your favorite neighbor's yard. Play Tug, give treats.

- Walk past a playground while kids are out running and playing. Say in a happy voice, "Do you hear those *kids*? Those are *kids, playing!*" Then offer a tiny piece of hot dog.

- Bring puppy to your friends' houses. If puppy's not potty trained yet, walk around out front until puppy goes to the bathroom, then visit inside for just five minutes — ideally long enough for your happy voices to encourage the puppy to investigate your friend's lap as she sits on the floor.

- Once puppy's comfortable trotting along on a leash, go for walks in increasingly busy environments where pup can encounter — at a distance if need be — all kinds of people, other dogs, and vehicles. Take it gradually: hitting Main Street on a busy, sunny Saturday is not the way to start. Start out a few streets from the center of town, and pick a quiet time.

- Take your pup on lots of short, predictable car rides. Going around the block is good, and going someplace the puppy loves is even better. Don't let the only car rides be to the vet.

- Give pup a chance to try walking on all kinds of different surfaces: grass, sand, mud, concrete, tile, stairs, a bridge. Remember, no forcing! Just present the opportunity, give it time, and toss a piece of chicken once that step is taken.

- Give your pup a chance to step in water. Small streams on a woods walk are a great way to start.

Don't Get Overwhelmed!

I hope that, after reading this long chapter, you feel empowered rather than overwhelmed. Once you wrap your head around effective socialization, it's actually easy to give your pup (and yourself) this amazing gift. It does not take loads of time — it's really a matter of flipping a switch so that you keep it top of mind.

Happen to have lots of time this evening? Bring your pup to your friend's house. Overwhelmed by other obligations today? Fine. Just put on a hat!

18

OTHER DOGS

Build Your Pup a Friendly Canine World

Creating the right canine social circle for your puppy in the first few months of his life will pay great rewards. Your pup will be happier, much easier to be around, and primed to be the kind of adult dog who gets along with other dogs.

Puppies thrive when they can interact with their own kind — like-minded individuals who understand that it makes sense to sniff one another's privates or play a bit of bitey-face. After all, we've taken them from their wrestling, chasing, jumping littermates and plunked them down on Planet Human. That transition is much easier if they have some fellow travelers.

Be careful, though, because for the youngest of puppies, interacting with other dogs does carry risk. In the key "socialization window" before the age of four months — during which it is critically important that a puppy experiences new things in a way that feels positive — the distemper-parvo vaccination series is not yet complete. A pup of that age who is around a sick dog is at risk of catching a life-threatening disease. (See chapter 16.)

As scary as that sounds, making nuanced choices to avoid disease is actually the easy part of getting dog-to-dog socialization right. The trickier part to navigate is that perfectly healthy dogs can pose a risk to puppies, too. They might hurt the pups physically, or they might simply scare them with their exuberance, their rough play, or their vocalizations. That psychological impact can be particularly damaging during the sponge-like, sensitive period of development before four months of age.

Even though it might seem much easier to just wait until later when the puppy is fully vaccinated and not so easily imprinted upon, that's a mistake. After this developmental stage, a puppy is more apt to see new and unknown things as a threat. That's why a pup who's isolated until emerging fully vaccinated at five months may be forever unable to feel truly comfortable around other dogs. (I hate to freak you out like this, but I do want to convey that socialization is an immediate priority.)

So, yes, it takes effort to introduce your pup safely to other dogs, but it's worth it. Plus, doggy interactions are a very fun part of socializing a puppy. Just get yourself up to speed on how to plan a safe and positive experience, and you're on your way to seeing a whole new side of your pup.

The Benefits of a Puppy Playdate

If you have a puppy who seems all teeth, please put "Find a great puppy playmate" at the top of your to-do list. If you — or your young kids — are having trouble finding a pain-free way to interact with your bitey pup, the puppy playdate can be a godsend.

A little half-hour romp with the neighbor's puppy can do four giant things:

1. Give your puppy a natural outlet for those mouthy impulses

2. Truly tire her out, which results in a puppy who's no longer all teeth

3. Build your puppy's doggy communication skills

4. Teach the important "bite inhibition" that will make her safer to be around as an adult dog

Safe Playmates, Good Setups

To find the right playmate, think safety first. Look for well-informed humans who are responsible and who keep their not-fully-vaccinated puppy away from unknown dogs and the places they frequent (like dog parks). Have a chat about how crucial it is to cancel any playdate if a puppy isn't in tip-top shape that day.

Once you have a puppy playdate scheduled, think about the location. You want to set things up so that each puppy feels safe and can choose whether or not to interact throughout the whole play-date. The environment can help a great deal with this, so arrange for your yard or room to have hiding places and obstacles that slow play and offer a breather: benches, bushes, or furniture to go over and under. If you offer just an empty space, it will usually end up with one puppy feeling cornered and scared, which is the opposite of what we're trying to accomplish.

When and How to Intervene

Even with a great setup, you'll need to intervene in the puppies' play at times. The key is knowing when and how. Especially at the beginning of the playdate, you may see behavior signaling that the pups need some help figuring out how to play well together: maybe one pup is repeatedly standing stiffly over another, or their wrestling turns into a very vocal, snappy skirmish. Be careful not to add to the puppies' uncertainty by hovering nervously and offering negative commentary. The dreaded "Be niiice," delivered in a weirdly threatening tone, will just freak the dogs out. They have no idea what you mean: all they know is that you are suddenly nervous, and they will associate that anxiety with this other puppy.

Instead, use your positive vibe to make things better. Remember that puppies are basically very distractible toddlers. Jump in with a cheery "Chase me, puppies! Look at this long rope!" Call them over for a chance to Sit for a piece of yummy cheese, and Touch for a bite of hot dog. Clap your hands and encourage them to join you on a little perimeter hike as you investigate the area together. These side-by-side activities help to decrease the intensity between them, so that when they engage again, things are calmer. Encouraging them to play Tug with a long toy — instead of constantly using those teeth on each other — can also help things stay positive.

If you're not sure how things are going, look for reciprocal play. It's ideal if pups are trading off who's chasing whom, who's on top, or who has the ball. If it's not looking very balanced, use the consent test. Calmly separate the pups, and see if the one that looked more hesitant seeks out play again. If they both pull wildly to be together again, then game on! If not, then it's time to try something else — maybe a walk together on leashes.

If this sounds like a lot of work, you're right! But it gets much, much better. It's typical to need a lot of human intervention on the first playdate between two pups, and almost none by the fourth. That's because, when you do it right, the puppies build their friendship, their communication skills, their play repertoire, and their confidence to the point where they can entertain each other happily. Even better, once they learn to do that with one friend, the process will likely go much more quickly with the next.

Many dog training facilities now offer puppy play sessions. These can be great — but you need to do your homework. What precautions do they take about health? Ask if you can watch a session beforehand. Are humans intervening well to promote better play? I have had several clients come to me convinced their puppy is a social misfit based on commentary from the employee in charge of a group session. Most of the time, that human was tasked with an impossible situation (too many puppies, the wrong mix of puppies, an inappropriate space) and wasn't able to create a good scenario for all of the puppies. With an appropriate setup, the pups who previously got a poor report card usually do beautifully.

(More detail in chapter 21.)

Strangers' Dogs on Leashes

As important as puppy friends are, they're just the beginning of your dog-to-dog socialization project. Your puppy will benefit tremendously from exposure to adult dogs too. Even seeing dogs walking on the other side of the street can be great for your puppy. When your pup notices the other dog, narrate for him: "Hey, see that dog? I see a dog." And then just move along. The best reaction your puppy can have to seeing an unknown dog while out and about is "Ho-hum. That's just a dog. No biggie."

Please don't let your pup go right up and greet a stranger's dog. You just don't know how that's going to go. Many adult dogs feel uncomfortable around puppy energy, which is perfectly reasonable, since it typically features "rude" jumping, climbing, and mouthing. Bad things can happen if a dog is taken aback by your puppy.

On the other hand, some of those stranger dogs may be happily excited about meeting your puppy. That's not really much better. Their fast movements or aroused barking may terrify your pup. And you don't know if the stranger's dog is vaccinated, or if the stranger's assertion that her dog "loves puppies" is accurate. So choose to be safe, and pass unknown dogs with a cheery attitude, keeping your distance. Sure, the encounter might go okay. But if it doesn't, you may end up with a puppy who is forever scared of other dogs.

Walks with Neighbor Dogs

A much better prospect for interaction is the calm dog who belongs to your nice, responsible, pet-vaccinating neighbors. Maybe nobody's sure how that dog might feel about a puppy, but it's worth finding out.

A great way to get those two dogs used to each other is to take a joint walk, with each owner carrying plenty of treats to keep things moving forward. Keep some distance between the dogs and let them size each other up as they move along on an adventure. After a bit, if the body language from the adult dog is all good (loose and waggy) and the puppy is leaning in to the experience, you can allow closer contact. Be careful not to let the leashes get tangled, which can make a dog feel trapped and cause a bad reaction.

Another possibility for a first introduction is to use a fence, a gate, or a pen to keep the puppy safe as the two dogs sniff each other. Again, use rapid treat delivery on both sides to lessen the intensity of the interaction between them at first. Ask for Sits and Touches as they get used to being around each other.

Even if you never get to the point of feeling comfortable allowing free play between that neighbor dog and your puppy, this can be a really helpful relationship. A wonderful role an older dog can play is to get a young puppy going on a walk. Often younger puppies don't want to leave their property, but if a nice old Lab leads the way, they'll suddenly trot along. (But don't let the puppy harass the older dog — pay attention to the body language of both, and keep some distance when needed.)

The Wonderful Nanny Dog

If you're lucky, somewhere in your neighborhood or your social circle there is a nanny dog. This is the adult dog who is eager to hang out with puppies, happy to patiently absorb the jumpy/mouthy chaos that is an excited three-month-old. These dogs can gently teach a pup boundaries — like "That biting is too hard" or "I'm done now" — which will make that pup forever safer with other dogs. Nanny dogs are absolute gold. If you have access to one, make the most of it, and schedule regular get-togethers.

This doesn't mean you should ever trap an older dog — even a perfectly patient one — with a puppy in the hopes that they'll "teach them some manners." The type of teaching we hope for can only happen when the older dog is voluntarily choosing to be around the puppy. Even a nanny dog sometimes needs a break, so be sure to give him the ability to hop over a low bench or up on a high sofa to escape the little wild thing. Also, don't hamper his ability to teach by disciplining the growl ("Be niiice"), because the growl is simply communication. The older dog needs to be able to say "nope" or else it's just not fair to pair him with a rude puppy. When I'm supervising — as one should always be in this situation — I back up my nanny dog's growl by quietly, calmly saying, "That's right, Georgie, good job." Then I might step in and help move things in a good direction.

(Special note: whenever two dogs are together, watch for "resource guarding," which can lead to real conflict if one dog tries to take an object from the other. If you see signs of difficulty, simply remove prized toys or other items, and often those dogs can resume hanging out happily together.)

Set Expectations about Interactions

If you happen to live in a wonderfully friendly neighborhood, where everybody knows each other and there are dozens of lovely dogs who always say hello on walks — I'm so sorry. While that's a fantastic vibe for a street, it creates an expectation in your puppy that it's normal to say hello to every single dog she sees out on a walk. It may be darling to see your eleven-week-old pulling on the leash to greet her friends, but later on that's likely to be a problem. Six months later, as you walk down Main Street, your seventy-pound adolescent is pulling madly toward every dog she sees and barking in frustration when she isn't allowed to gallop over to say hello.

To combat that, my favorite approach is to teach a puppy that unless she hears a special cue, like "Go say hello," leashed dogs are just things we pass by calmly, sometimes getting a treat. So if I lived in that super-friendly neighborhood, I'd control the early exposure to other dogs. I'd invite those great neighbor dogs for playdates and planned walks together, but particularly in the beginning, I'd teach my pup to walk past them nicely when we randomly encounter them on walks.

Other dogs can play a transformative role in your puppy's early development. They can make a puppy feel less lonely here on Planet Human, they can offer a fun and easy way to burn off energy in play, and they can model and teach behavior that'll make your puppy's life happier and safer. For sure it takes time and effort to bring those dogs safely into your puppy's orbit, but the payoff is enormous for both of you.

19

BODY LANGUAGE

Learn to Spot These Subtle Clues

The key to socializing effectively is using your puppy's feelings as a guide, but that's impossible if you don't know how your dog is feeling. Studying up on canine body language is the answer. A few indicators are obvious — trembling, running away, hiding — but it's really the more subtle signs that you'll be using every day. Here's a quick rundown.

Turning or leaning away. If you are approaching (or petting and hugging) a dog and he turns his head away, pay attention. That's likely a polite request for space. A dog who actually wants that attention will turn toward it and lean in. Not sure? Then back up a bit, put your hands behind your back, and see if pup comes to initiate contact.

Yawns. Tired puppies tend to simply conk out or act wild. They don't sit around yawning. A yawn is much more often a sign of stress. You'll see it in a training class, you'll see it when guests come over, you'll see it if you're petting too much, and you'll see it when kids hug a dog. If you see a yawn, ask yourself what might be stressing your dog.

Rolling over. Yes, sometimes happy dogs will roll over to invite a belly rub. But rolling over and exposing the belly can also be a white flag, a sign the dog feels overwhelmed. Additional context clues can tell you which you're seeing, but it's best to err on the side of caution. Back up five feet, sit on the ground (so you're not looming), and give the dog the space and time to make his own decision. (If the rolling over happens when your puppy is surrounded by your kid's squealing soccer team, that's probably not a request for a belly rub.)

Stillness or sleep. Sometimes people tell me their puppy was "amazing" at the [big, chaotic experience that the human couldn't have dialed back to meet the puppy's needs]. "She slept the whole time!" "He just sat still while everybody petted him!" Just like human babies, puppies sometimes escape by going to sleep when they're feeling overwhelmed. Sometimes they will just sit or lie very still, feeling they have no other choice. Humans misinterpret this as "good as gold" behavior when it is actually a sign of fear.

Lip licking. As with yawning, dogs sometimes lick their lips when they feel uncomfortable. (Also, of course, when there's peanut butter on them.)

"Kiss to dismiss." When dogs lick humans with affection, it's typically one quick flick, or a long, slow series of leisurely, soft licks. But the lick that is worrisome — the one that behaviorists have dubbed the "kiss to dismiss" — looks different. It's intense, sometimes becoming fast, hard, and even frantic. Parents of small children often misinterpret this behavior as a sign the dog is finally learning to love their toddler, when in fact that licking is intended to politely get that small, advancing human to back off. I know it sounds impossible to tell the difference, so just be aware that this is a possibility. As always, if you're not sure, give pup some easy, no-stress distance from the kissee and watch what happens.

Facial tension. A wrinkled forehead sure is cute on a puppy — until you realize those wrinkles are exaggerated because the pup is so worried. A mouth that's tightly clamped shut echoes the message of those wrinkles.

"Whale eye." When trainers see too much of the white of a dog's eye, they look to see what might be wrong. That "whale eye" can be a sign that the dog is stressed out, staying very still but moving the eyes to watch what's happening. (A relaxed dog would simply turn her head.)

This list is not intended to make you throw up your hands and ask how on earth you're supposed to read your dog's body language. It's designed to help you get started learning and observing. Your puppy's so very lucky to have you reading this far! (Want to dive in? Lili Chin's book *Doggie Language* is fantastic. See Recommendations and Resources.)

20

NARRATING PLANET HUMAN

Talk to Your Puppy

As you introduce your puppy to the wider world, you're going to get some funny looks from people if you're doing it right. That's because you'll be talking — a lot — to a dog.

My four-month-old pup Georgie and I were happily walking through our local park when something mysterious stopped him in his tracks: a flying kite. His body language — lowered head, ready-to-flee crouch — telegraphed, "What the heck is that?" Pulling out my favorite fancy dog-trainer trick to get him through this moment, I said, "Georgie, it's okay! It's just a bird."

This had two immediate results: (1) a relaxed, confident, bouncy trot from Georgie toward the kite, and (2) a look that said, "That lady's crazy" on the face of the little boy flying the kite with his dad.

I laughed and told the humans that I do indeed know the difference between a kite and a bird, but that this phrase helped my dog to understand, "Ah, so that's a thing that flies around that we don't have to worry about."

"Huh," said the dad. "I never thought about trying to teach my dog something like that." Me neither, Kite Dad. But when I took a canine applied ethology course, one of the top ten takeaways was the power of verbal narration. It's crazy how much words can help dogs navigate this confusing human world.

I've always talked to my dogs, as most of us do. But thanks to Kim Brophey, an ethologist turned dog behaviorist, I now consciously name things for dogs in a way that gives them a clue about what's coming next. Naming the things a dog may view negatively turns out to ease anxiety (along with its cousins skittishness and reactivity) fairly dramatically.

Yes, I'm asking you to talk to your puppy more. It sounds too simple, but I promise you, it's a game changer.

The Mister Rogers Hack

It turns out that dogs have a receptive language ability on a par with a toddler's. As Brophey delved into this topic during her week-long course, a light bulb went on for me. I taught preschool before I pivoted to dogs, and I can tell you that while most toddlers can't articulate their thoughts very well, they understand an astounding percentage of what people say.

We make an effort to tell those toddlers what's going on around them, which builds their confidence and helps them to see patterns in an otherwise chaotic world. Think about the old show *Mister Rogers' Neighborhood* and that dear man's reassuring commentary: "Let's go over to the tank and feed the fish now."

That purposeful narration works for dogs too, and Brophey calls it her "Mister Rogers Hack." She explains that because so much of our human environment is utterly foreign to dogs, they're constantly having to work hard figuring out what the heck is going on. "Should I be worried? Should I be excited? Will I be interacting with that? Will it be loud? Can I eat it?" Cue the anxiety, skittishness, arousal, and reactivity.

We can lessen their load by explaining life as it unfolds, just as Mister Rogers does.

This does not mean that we should all begin babbling to our dogs about, say, global politics. The key to this hack is that the oft-repeated words and phrases must be meaningful for the dog. When related to things the dog has feelings about, the Mister Rogers Hack gives the dog a clue about what's coming next, helping him to prepare.

For example, the other day I was walking my three big dogs, and we turned a corner to find a construction crew working on the street. A handful of men were wearing reflective gear and hard hats, holding big tools, and working next to a noisy truck. If I had done nothing at that moment I'd have had a challenge on my hands: one barker, one slinker, and a hundred-pound adolescent open to suggestion. Historically, my approach would have been to (1) switch direction or (2) use cues like Touch, Look, and Find It to pull the dogs' attention away from the crew and back to something familiar and reassuring as we passed by as quickly as we could. With three of them, though, that's not always a graceful moment.

So I used the Mister Rogers Hack, as I'd been doing for the past few months. I exclaimed in a cheery voice, "Oh, great, they're *fixing* it!" My dogs relaxed. No stream of cues necessary. No distraction necessary. They were able to casually watch the crew as we loose-leashed our way past. That's because now I always use that phrase — "Oh, great, they're *fixing* it!" — when there are unexpected humans working in unusual places, doing strange, loud things in weird clothing.

The phrase "They're *fixing* it!" allows my dogs' brains to stop working so hard to figure out every single construction, lawn care, painting, or tree-trimming crew we come across. Those words help my dogs to categorize this experience because it's part of a pattern they can recognize. They can now predict what's next: we'll continue our walk, and that temporary crew won't impact us.

Sample Vocabulary

Using a word to indicate a category of things that will just pass on by is incredibly helpful, relaxing information for a human to supply. Here are examples of words that, when used regularly, can reduce arousal and anxiety by communicating to your dog that (a) you see the thing too and (b) it won't affect the pair of you at all:

Plane = anything loud in the sky

Bike = human moving fast on a nonmotorized bike, scooter, or skateboard

Neighbor = random person we see out walking

Kids playing = kids moving around, being loud

Runner = a human moving fast

Doggy = a dog we see but won't greet up close

You can use words like these to give your dog a heads-up to anticipate more interaction:

Buddy = a dog we'll get up close to, sniff, or walk or play with

Friend = a human we'll say hi to

Guest = someone coming into the house (a word telegraphing that people will come in, sit around, and talk)

Helper = a plumber, electrician, painter, or anybody coming onto the property to work, likely hanging out for a while, perhaps unsupervised by family, using tools, and making noise

It can be helpful (and just plain fun) to teach your dog words to explain activities that come up every day, like these:

TV time! = snuggle in, because we'll be here for a while

See ya later = go ahead and nap, because I'm leaving for a while

I'll be right back = don't follow me upstairs, because I'm coming immediately back down

This way = we're going to change direction

This simple shift in how we talk to our dogs is one of the biggest gifts we can give them. Intentional, consistent, predictive narration creates calmer dogs. The bonus? Happier humans — even if it does mean you get a funny look from a stranger when you call a kite a bird.

21

PUPPY FRIENDS

Plan and Supervise Great Playdates

If there's one thing that can serve as the Magic Elixir of puppyhood, it's the puppy playdate. Half an hour spent wrestling and chasing with the right canine friends will have an enormous payoff in both the short and the long term. However, making sure these experiences are positive takes some forethought.

You're Not Off Duty

Playdate rule 1 is that the humans are very much on duty during the initial stages of this hoped-for friendship. While it's true that a first playdate will buy you some time off, that payoff only comes afterward, when your pup snores in his crate for two hours. (Later playdates between true friends don't need as much supervision, so they really are time off for you.) During the first playdate, you'll need to be switched on. If your plan is to let the puppies "work it out themselves," you're better off skipping the experience, because it could backfire completely. Instead, be ready to help your pup navigate this new situation.

The introduction is key. If possible, let the puppies say hello through a gate or a fence. That way there can be lots of informative sniffing without either pup getting physically overwhelmed. You'll be tempted to be polite and talk with the other human, but your puppy may need your support as she figures out this new scenario. Stick close as you keep up your own cheery narration: "Look! It's a buddy! We can play!" After a minute or two, or ten, when it's clear from their body language that both puppies are interested in more interaction — nobody is shrinking away or pretending the other dog doesn't exist — you can remove the barrier. You might keep a leash on the more confident pup for a bit in order to give the other pup more space at first. Once you see more confidence and interest, pop off that leash.

Great playdates happen when humans are keen observers. So, what are you looking for? Ideally, you'll see some loose, waggy bodies, a play-bow, and reciprocal action where the chaser becomes the chasee, and the top wrestler takes a turn on the bottom. In contrast, stiff bodies and cornered dogs signal that it's time for you to jump in to help.

Wonderful doggy play can look a little scary to the uninitiated human. If two pups are interacting in a way that concerns you, gently take the pups apart and give them a moment to regroup. Then let go. Do they happily seek each other out, or does one of them run for the hills? If they both keep choosing to engage, that's a sign it's all good.

If a pup consistently heads toward the gate where he came in, or is lying down there, it's a sign that he needs help engaging happily, or that it's time to head home and try again another day.

How to Intervene: Motion and Training

If you need to step in and help the pups interact, your tools are motion, redirection, and a fun training session in which each pup can earn treats for easy Sits and Touches.

- **Walk!** Lead a parade around the perimeter. Clap your hands, call the puppies, and start a group hike. Pups who were, just moments earlier, heading toward a too-intense interaction can suddenly be very companionable as they move together in the same direction, no longer intensely focused on each other but instead sharing the discovery of new things to smell. I sometimes spend the entire first half hour of my puppy socialization class walking half a dozen puppies around the perimeter of the yard. This gives them a chance to size each other up, so that they feel more confident in one another's presence, and burns off a bit of energy. They're ready to play.

- **Redirect!** Redirect any undesired play into something better. Introduce new elements — a ball to chase, a squeaky toy, a baby pool — to distract pups and lead them into different behaviors. A quick, happy interruption can work wonders. Mind you, we aren't "correcting" behavior here. We're not using scary voices or a big "No" with pups who are already perhaps confused and overwhelmed. Instead we confidently, cheerily draw them onto a new path.

- **Ask for Sits!** Do some training. Call the pups and reward them for some quick Sits, Spins, or Touches before sending them back to play. It's a great idea to do this a handful of times during every playdate, but especially when things seem to be veering away from mutually fun play. It can be reassuring to a nervous dog, and a solid reminder for a confident dog, that listening to you is the most reliable route to the best things in life. If the playdate has felt at all chaotic or confusing to a young pup, a predictable little training moment can help settle him.

When you're handing out treats during a playdate, keep in mind that dogs often won't take treats well in a group, and that itself can lead to a kerfuffle. Get more humans to help if necessary, or hold your hands far apart as you reward the puppies simultaneously. Very quickly, they learn that each pup will get their fair share and that sitting nicely without grabbing is the fastest path to the treat. I am careful to clearly articulate each pup's name and wait for eye contact before I put that treat in his mouth, and it's amazing how quickly that helps a whole group of pups understand, "Oh, that one's not for me. I need to wait for my name."

When to Use Toys — and When Not To

If play seems a notch too intense, it often helps to incorporate a toy. It provides just a bit of distance and a safe target for teeth. However, many dogs need to be taught how to use toys with their friends. Once you help get them going by dangling, tugging, and throwing, it is darling to watch them brandish a toy near a friend, luring them into a new game.

Every now and then there's a young pup whose natural resource-guarding instincts really kick in around toys. In that case, it's best to pop the prized items out of sight for that day.

Yard Setup

A private, fenced yard is the ideal puppy playdate setting. It allows you to control which dogs make the guest list and also to minimize health risks. (Much-used public areas are more likely to have yucky things like coccidia or giardia lurking in the grass.)

There are ways to make your space conducive to good play. A big, flat, empty square spells trouble! If one pup feels there's no-where to hide, and no place to catch his breath, he may decide he has no choice but to stand his ground fiercely, thus creating a wholly unnecessary point of stress.

If you're lucky enough to have a yard with lots of (sturdy!) bushes and trees, that's great. But if you don't, simply adding some low tables, benches, planters, and an elevated dog bed can help create a great dynamic. In a pinch, a bunch of big cardboard boxes could help. Pups need a place to take temporary refuge from the action. It's okay if your puppy runs to hide under the bench, as long as pretty soon you see her popping her head out, eager to get involved again. In addition to providing resting spots, the extra elements allow a pup who otherwise might have been intimidated into a corner to lead a very fun over-and-under-and-around game of chase. The more familiar the dogs get with the layout of a yard with all sorts of ins and outs, the more fun — and enriching — those chase games become.

Guest List

Now that you know how to approach a playdate, which puppies do you invite? (Of course, before puppies have completed their distemper-parvo vaccination series, the first qualifier for the potential puppy friend is responsible, informed ownership. See chapter 16.)

When you give your puppy time with all kinds of dogs (chasers and wrestlers, the pointy-eared and the floppy-eared), she becomes fluent in various styles of play and communication. That works as an inoculation against future fear-driven freak-outs resulting from canine misunderstandings. As you try to expand your list of playmates, however, you'll want to consider size and age. Too big a discrepancy can lead to unintentional injuries.

Keeping a leash on a bigger or more experienced pup at first can give a smaller or younger dog a chance to size up the situation and to communicate with the big pup without being overwhelmed. But the sooner leashes can safely come off, the better, because of course they do alter behavior and sometimes add unhelpful frustration.

If there's a big size discrepancy between two dogs you'd really like to have as pals, indoor play can be an answer. A seventy-pound teenage Lab mix can sometimes do beautifully with a fifteen-pound three-month-old in the family room, where they'll do some mouthy wrestling. That same pairing could be dangerous outside in a big yard if the big pup gets up speed and bowls the little one over.

It's simplest to start with pups who are close in age and size. After that, be prepared to watch closely and use your best judgment. Some big dogs are geniuses at playing gently, while plenty of medium-sized dogs have such rough styles that they need to play with bigger dogs to be safe. Keen observation is the key.

How Long Should a Playdate Be?

If you're trying to get the biggest bang for your buck, a twenty-minute playdate is perfect. It takes only twenty of your minutes, but every single one of them can be wonderfully enriching (and exhausting, in a good way) for your dog. If that's all you can squeeze in, don't worry! If every dog on the planet had a daily twenty-minute playdate with a good friend down the block, the number of anxious, destructive, and aggressive dogs would plummet.

My favorite playdates are longer, though, especially if playmates are new to each other. As sessions stretch past the twenty-minute mark, you'll start to see the best play of all. Confidence grows as the overabundance of energy diminishes. As trust builds between dogs, they start to figure out what they like to do together. Sometimes pups who seemed like a poor match after twenty minutes are playing beautifully after forty.

Conversely, sometimes pups who've been doing well suddenly get snappish. That can simply mean they're tired and it's time to call it a day. The newer the relationships, the more stimulating (and exhausting) the event will be. Here's the key (I know you can guess it by now): observe closely, and you'll know when it's time to call it quits.

Why Make the Effort?

A playdate is work. But on the simplest, most practical level, a great playdate can be a godsend for humans dealing with a jumpy, mouthy pup who can't seem to focus. Just like recess at school, allowing a little one to expend energy in an acceptable way helps her to settle down to listen and learn. Especially for families with young children at home, a vigorous puppy playdate can make their new furry alligator much more pleasant to be around.

Those short-term gains feel huge at the time, but for me (the one *not* living day to day with that pup) the most important benefits of playdates are the long-term ones. A young pup who has regular positive playdates with a handful of different friends, ideally in a variety of settings, is set up to be a more confident, safer dog — *forever*. His repertoire of doggy communication skills will make him a canine diplomat, able to diffuse tension and avoid fights. He will develop the critical "bite inhibition" that keeps dogs from biting hard. Mouthing is a huge part of doggy play, but pups who bite too hard discover that their playmates don't like it, so they learn to calibrate that grip. That lesson comes in handy when your Aunt Matilda steps on your adult dog's tail and his head whips around in surprise. A pup who hasn't learned bite inhibition from his doggy friends is more likely to just sink those teeth right in.

When playdates involve a handful of different yards and humans, the puppy's world expands. The pup learns to anticipate good things in association with a new place and with strangers. If playdates involve a quick car ride, even better! The pup will learn to associate the car with happy experiences. Finally, hosting playdates at home teaches a pup that it's great to have people and dogs over. Many folks who adopted puppies during the lockdown phases of the Covid-19 pandemic later learned just how hard it is for an adult dog to get used to the idea of guests. If you can host during puppyhood, do it.

PART 5

BEHAVIOR

22

BEYOND TRAINING

Five Key Themes for Great Behavior

Most of my clients tell me they want their puppy to grow up to be a dog who's easy to live with, one who doesn't have problematic behaviors. They describe this as a "well-trained dog."

I think of that as a "well-understood dog."

It's a critical difference, because it affects where you put your energy. If you spend lots of hours training but little time understanding who your dog really is, you probably won't get the result you're after.

Don't get me wrong: training (which I think of as intentionally setting out to teach a particular behavior or skill) plays an important role in ending up with a dog who's a great companion. It gives you a shared vocabulary, tools for navigating new situations, and (when done right) it dramatically builds your bond. Training is the biggest section in this book, and I hope you'll dive into it.

But teaching the dog what *we* want to see will come up short in the end if it isn't grounded in a larger approach that considers the dog's needs, too. To set the stage for behavior that's easy to live with, you have to think *beyond* training. Switching your mindset from "We have to train the puppy" to "We need to understand the puppy" is gold.

What exactly do I mean by "beyond" training? It's the five critical themes below: *safety, enrichment, agency, observation,* and *management.* They work together to ease a puppy's transition to Planet Human, and when they are fully in play, problem behaviors rarely have a chance to develop. Anchor your dog's puppyhood in these things (woven into all the advice in this book), and you will be well on your way to the dog of your dreams, no matter how much official "training" you do.

1. **Provide a sense of safety.** Life with humans can be confusing and even terrifying for a new pup from Planet Dog. Helping a puppy to feel secure in various conditions and environments is a human's number one job, and doing it well can be transformative in terms of behavior.

2. **Meet canine needs through enrichment.** Here on Planet Human we sometimes describe dogs as spoiled when they have fancy beds, custom collars, and expensive toys. But they don't need that stuff. Instead, they have fundamental Planet Dog needs that are often ignored. When you find a way to regularly let a dog be a dog — sniffing, chewing, chasing, barking, digging — "problem" behaviors often magically disappear.

3. **Allow a sense of agency.** Pet dogs in today's society typically don't have much say in their own lives compared to even fifty years ago. These days, most dogs are some combination of controlled, directed, leashed, crated, confined, indoors, and alone for enormous portions of their day. Think about that for a moment. Then ponder the power you have and use it to give your dog some choice. For example, let your dog sniff that fascinating spot for a long time, rather than pulling on the leash and saying, "There's nothing there!" (Of course there *is* something there, something our pathetic human nasal receptors simply can't detect.) Little moments throughout the day like that add up, for better or for worse. Giving your dog a sense of agency in this way can dramatically reduce anxiety and build confidence. Bonus: if you give her a chance to tell you the things she loves to do, sniff, eat, look at, and play with, rather than making all of those decisions yourself, you'll get to know your real dog.

4. **Take time to observe.** We're all so busy that we rarely sit back and observe our dogs. That's a mistake. Slow down, stop directing, watch, and learn. Become an expert in your dog's body language. The answers to your biggest frustrations may be right in front of you.

5. **Use management to help your pup succeed.** To the surprise of their clients, the first recommendation of great trainers is often management: thoughtful anticipation, combined with limited choices. Somehow our society has created the belief that a good dog should be able to handle any situation. That's utterly unfair and sets dogs up for failure. Instead, it's our job to understand what's challenging for our individual pets and to protect them by limiting their ability to screw up. (Pup getting into the bathroom trash? Get one of those little cans with a pedal-operated lid. Done.) Training is great, but when the behavior has to be perfect, responsible owners turn to management. Want proof? No group of people has more gates stashed throughout their homes than trainers.

Want your dog to act well trained? Start by making sure your puppy is well understood. The rest will follow.

23

THE GOLDEN RULE

Catch Your Puppy Doing Something Right

It may sound too simple, but the best dog-behavior tip out there is this: catch your puppy doing something right.

We busy humans can easily get into a pattern of paying the most attention to our puppies when they've caused trouble. When they are acting exactly as we'd wish them to — lying peacefully on the dog bed while we cook, keeping four feet on the floor when guests arrive — our attention stays focused on the cooking or the guests. But if pup starts jumping up on folks, chewing the chair leg, or biting somebody's clothes, suddenly we find time to interact with her.

I beg you to reverse that dynamic. Tune in and notice when your puppy is doing what you'd love to see more of. Do it enough, and you'll start seeing a whole lot more of the behavior you want.

See-Mark-Reward Training

The "catch them doing something right" approach may intuitively make sense to you, and yet it will slip your mind during a busy day. The brilliant solution is the SMART × 50 method developed by the acclaimed behaviorist Kathy Sdao. The acronym stands for "see, mark, and reward training," and here's how it works:

- In the morning, count out fifty tiny treats. These could be kibble or something more exciting, like bacon-flavored training tidbits.

- Put them in a container where you'll see it and be reminded to play the game.

- Use them, one by one, to reward your puppy every time you see her doing something good *on her own*, without you asking for it.

- Mark the behavior with a calm "Yes" or "Good," then follow with a low-excitement delivery of the treat. Don't be so enthusiastic you pull your dog out of that nice, relaxed behavior.

- Make sure that jar is empty by the end of the day.

Result? Puppies get continual feedback about their own natural dog behaviors that work on Planet Human; humans are reminded to notice the good behavior in their dogs over and over, until they hit fifty examples a day where the pup made a choice that makes him easy to live with. A funny thing happens when you start to look for the good: there's more and more of it.

Putting SMART × 50 into Action

Here's what a SMART × 50 day might look like. Sure, at some point your puppy was chewing the sofa, and admittedly, you do have those muddy paw prints on your shirt. But you're not in an angry swirl, because there were fifty(!) times you noticed your puppy was:

- lying calmly on his bed during your Zoom call

- checking in with you using eye contact during a walk

- lying calmly on his mat while you cooked dinner

- keeping four feet on the floor when somebody entered the house

- lying calmly at your feet while you read to the kids

- sitting quietly nearby while you fed the cat

- lying calmly at your feet while you chatted with the neighbor

- making eye contact with you while you waited at the vet
- meandering into her crate on her own

These seemingly small, naturally occurring behaviors are gold. Ignoring them — as it is human nature to do — is a heartbreaking mistake. These moments, handled right, make a trail of breadcrumbs leading your puppy home. He needs clues to make sense of our silly human world, where jumping and mouthing and barking are — oddly, to him — not prized.

Seeing "Bad" Behavior Fade Away

A puppy who is lying quietly, sitting peacefully, or keeping four on the floor is very likely *not* pulling, chewing furniture, counter surfing, or doing any of the other things that people ask dog trainers like me to "fix."

Catching your dog doing something right is the easiest, cheapest training available. It takes no planning. There is no setup. You don't have to think, "Oh I should go train with the puppy." You don't have to find the time to go to classes. It's as easy as filling a jar and paying attention.

But for me, the best thing about SMART × 50 is the fundamental shift it creates in a human's head and heart. The old mindset is that your dog needs heavy-handed training so he "does what you want." With the SMART × 50 approach, you're taking a step back, appreciating that you're living with a different species, and making allowances for that. Then you're making the most of the moments when your wishes and your dog's choices go hand-in-paw — and building on that synergy to create a rewarding life together.

If that sounds too touchy-feely to you, consider this: my clients tell me nothing has ever worked faster to get them the behavior they wanted to see.

(For more on Kathy Sdao and SMART × 50, check out the first episode of my podcast *Pick of the Litter*.)

24

A PLEA FOR EMPATHY

Stop Saying No

Sometimes people tell me they need help because their puppy "just doesn't understand the word *no*." Their instinct is to become more punitive (say it louder! sound meaner! stomp off!) to make the meaning of the word clearer.

Do you ever wonder what it feels like to be a puppy — born with very strong instincts to jump, dig, chase, bark, and chew — and to have everyone mad at you all the time for being who you are? To hear "No" all day long, everywhere you turn? In your own home?

Instead of letting our kidnapped puppies stumble around bumping into all of the mystifying "No's" on Planet Human, let's give them a brightly lit path to "Yes." If you find you're saying "No" a lot, take a deep breath and sit down with a cup of tea and this book. Then make a list of things you can do to set your puppy up for success.

25

ESSENTIAL ENRICHMENT

Let Dogs Be Dogs

Is your puppy digging in the yard? Chewing the furniture? Pulling on lead with his nose to the ground? Those behaviors can be the observational breadcrumbs that will lead you to effective enrichment — and a much happier (and "well-behaved") dog.

Contrary to popular understanding, canine enrichment is not simply about providing something — anything — "extra." It is about meeting your own particular dog's needs by offering ways to engage in species-typical behaviors — behaviors that our modern way of life often does not allow. Canine enrichment helps dogs be dogs, and it can solve our human problems along the way.

Enrichment Started in Zoos

The concept of animal enrichment originated in the 1970s, as zoos were starting to focus on conservation. Breeding was a newly important goal — and it was proving elusive. Some began to theorize that the reason animals weren't procreating was that their daily life in captivity was too far from their norm in the wild. They weren't behaviorally, emotionally, or physically healthy enough to breed.

Some zoos experimented with ways to meet each animal's natural needs. Out went the standard, bare-bones enclosures, and in flooded perching areas, climbing vines, prey scents, hidden food, soundtracks of the wild, and more. The change brought dramatic success to breeding programs, but in addition it was an "aha!" moment. A new zoo focus was born: using behavior to assess health, and enrichment to improve it.

Unmet Needs Create Behavior Problems

The pet dog world was paying attention. Like the nonbreeding zoo animals, some pet dogs were showing — through increasing behavioral challenges — that something was off. Based on what was happening in zoos, behaviorists began to theorize that enrichment could make dogs more behaviorally sound, too. Rather than attempting to train the unwanted behavior out of the animal, they started looking at whether the dog's needs were being met.

"When you don't meet needs, you get maladaptive behaviors," says Emily Strong, who coauthored *Canine Enrichment for the Real World* with Allie Bender.

"What surprises people is that enrichment often solves behavior problems," says Bender. "When they have an issue, people assume they need a trainer, but nobody learns well when their needs aren't being met. So if the first step in a training plan focuses on meeting needs, sometimes the issues — jumping, barking, mouthing, digging, or whatever — simply go away."

Coming up with an enrichment plan for your dog starts with simple observation, and the *Canine Enrichment* authors encourage owners to "look with your eyes, not your ideas." That means watching your dog first, *then* coming up with a specific plan for enrichment. Note what your dog tends to want to do, and experiment with objects, activities, and ways to rearrange the environment that might scratch that itch.

Enrichment Ideas for Pullers, Counter Surfers, and Diggers

If your dog is pulling on the leash with her nose to the ground, she could have an unmet need for scenting. You might want to experiment with:

- adding more "sniffari" walks on which you go at the dog's pace, perhaps use a long lead, and seek out places that will be gloriously full of things to sniff: wildlife, other dogs, city life. (Some of the best enrichment options are free, like this one!)

- signing up for one of the scent-work classes that are popping up everywhere.
- creating your own scent-work adventures at home. (I saw a demonstration of this approach at a wolf sanctuary, where they put a tiny bit of pickle juice in the grass and the wolves spent fifteen minutes finding it, sniffing it, and rolling in it.)

Sure, you also want to work toward leash walks that are more pleasant for both of you by finding the right harness and working on engagement — but if an unmet need for scenting has been a factor in the puppy's pulling, those efforts will be more successful after this targeted enrichment.

If your dog is counter surfing, he could have an unmet need for foraging. You could experiment with:

- playing Find It on walks or while you're watching TV.
- using different food puzzles. (*Different* is important because it doesn't feel like foraging if the experience is exactly the same each time. Get creative. Hide that stuffed Toppl under the couch, then in the bathroom.)
- scatter feeding (both indoors and out) instead of feeding from bowls.

To address counter surfing it is also, of course, key to stop leaving delicious things unsupervised on the counter. But for a dog who's craving foraging, providing "legal" outlets for his instinctive behavior can make him much less obnoxious around food in general.

If your dog is digging, there are different unmet needs it could signify: maybe she's a terrier who needs to tunnel for rodents; maybe she's a beagle who needs to follow any scent to track the game; maybe she's a thick-coated husky who's just trying to reach cool dirt. You can experiment with the following:

• Provide a sandbox in a shady part of the yard, and hide toys in there.

• Make sure the pup has access to a cool surface like a tile floor, a raised dog bed with breathable fabric, or a crate bottom (some dogs hate it when you add cozy bedding). Be aware that the sun's position can heat up those nap spots during some parts of the day.

Enrichment as an Interesting Puzzle (for You)

The final part of the experiment is assessment. Is it really enrichment? You can only tell by watching your dog. Does he love it? Is he super-engaged? Has it decreased the problem behavior that led you to try this? If the answer is yes, that's enrichment. But if he leaves that Kong half filled or hides under your legs during that agility class, it's not functioning as enrichment, so it's time to think again. "The truth is, it's fun to solve these behavioral issues through enrichment," says Bender. "It's a rewarding puzzle."

"For me, thinking about enrichment flips the traditional mindset around dog behavior," says Strong. "Instead of thinking, 'What do I want the dog to do?,' we think, 'What does this dog need to do?' Oddly, when you do that, you often end up solving the first question."

26

QUICK THINKING

When the Puppy Absolutely Must "Drop It"

It's a perilous moment: You look over and see your puppy has something unusual in her mouth. Maybe it's valuable, like an expensive
new shoe. Maybe it's precious, like your son's favorite stuffed bear.
Or maybe it's dangerous, like a bottle of prescription meds. Whatever it is, you know it needs to come out of her mouth.

Quiz time. Which should you do?

1. Say, "Drop it!"
2. Chase the dog and get that item, no matter what.
3. Skip off in the opposite direction, jauntily singing a tune.

No pressure, but the approach you use might spell the difference between a dog who constantly looks for forbidden things to
pick up in her mouth (and possibly defend with a growl and worse)
and one who never develops that habit.

Hint: I hope you know how to skip and sing.

"Drop" or "Trade"

If you have already invested significant training time in teaching your
puppy that giving something up to you will pay off for her, you're
all set for this key moment. I suggest starting with the cue "Trade"
over "Drop" because its win-win nature makes it easier for new
puppy-owner teams to master. In a nutshell, you give the pup something good but not amazing to chew on, then you offer a particularly

enticing treat over to the side while you say, "Trade!" in a cheery voice. Pup will drop the chew to get the treat, so you calmly whisk the chew behind your back. The second the pup finishes swallowing the new treat and looks back at you, you happily present the chew from behind your back and say, "Take it!" Every time you practice this (maybe once or twice a week) pup gets the original item back, learning there is no downside to giving up a prized item.

If you've done that prep work, then in the scenario above, you can calmly use Trade, and your pup will relinquish the item. In this real-life use, you won't be giving it back, so be prepared to reward and distract the pup so well that Trade will still work the next time you have to use it.

The Yell-and-Grab

But what if you're not at that level yet? Without a solid Trade (or Drop) cue, most folks instinctively employ the yell-and-grab method, chasing down the pup and physically extracting the item from the puppy's mouth. After all, every second counts when it comes to either damage inflicted to the item or danger to the pup.

But is the yell-and-grab really the fastest, safest way to retrieve the item? It is not. Even if it works in this particular moment, you've set yourself up for trouble. Here are some likely unintended and unpleasant outcomes:

1. The pup is delighted with your newfound attention. "Game on!" Pup is thrilled you've finally looked up from that dreary computer work and realized there is fun to be had. Pup runs and scampers, staying just out of reach. You stay engaged. What did pup learn? "To have a super-happy time with Mom, just grab something that's not a puppy toy."

2. The pup is scared of your shockingly big, mad voice and fast movement, runs and hides, maybe under the couch. It takes a long time to get her, and the item, out. What did pup learn? "Don't ever trust Dad, because he's unpredictable."

3. Seeing your approach, puppy knows she has just seconds to work with, so she gobbles down the item instead of just playing with it, and now that chicken bone she found under the bush in the park is down her throat. What did pup learn? Nothing, but now you've got a big vet bill.

4. The pup begins to realize that you are constantly trying to steal her special treasures, so she goes on offense, growling and snapping. What has puppy learned? "These people take all the good stuff, so be ready to fend them off." This last issue is very serious. You may find out too late that you have inadvertently contributed to the creation of a resource guarder, and you'll need a good private trainer to help.

The Skip-and-Sing

Here's where we get to the skipping and singing. It is utterly counterintuitive, but if you have not taught a beautiful Trade or Drop, the best way to get the item back immediately is to give it exactly zero attention. If there's anything more enticing to a dog than a new thing, it's a new thing that somebody else wants. (Don't believe me? Watch a dog suddenly care about the stupid old bone she's never, ever chewed until the neighbor's dog comes over and picks it up.)

The second you see the item in your puppy's mouth, you spring into action — elsewhere! Make your puppy suddenly think that the item is worthless because (1) you aren't paying attention to it, and (2) you seem to be doing something else really exciting. Humans aren't the only ones who experience FOMO (fear of missing out).

Leap up. Skip to the kitchen singing the "I'm getting out the ham" song. Be goofy. This alone (provided it doesn't happen all the time) can be enough to startle your dog into dropping the item.

Do not run back to the scene of the crime, grab the item, and give a big lecture about how he's never to do this again. That will undo all your good work. Instead, give your future self a gift and prove to your dog that it always pays to see what you're up to when you're acting goofy. Ask for some Sits and Spins and Downs, and reward with that ham. Then scatter kibble on the floor so it'll take him a little while to find it all, slip out, and quietly pick up the item and put it out of reach. Phew! Done.

Another option is the treat trail. Take that ham and make a little path of ham bits starting right at your puppy's feet and heading away from the item. (You can't eat ham with prescription sunglasses in your mouth.)

Maybe for your Tug-obsessed dog, offering up that special tug toy will do the trick. Or for a dog obsessed with his canine buddy, maybe offering a trip next door to play with Jasper will suffice. Your own knowledge of your dog will help you figure out what will create the FOMO that will make him drop the item.

Boost Your Prevention Skills

Sometimes people hear the description of the skip-and-sing approach and say, "Come on! My puppy grabs stuff all day long! I can't do this whole shebang every single time."

Quiz time: What is wrong with the sentence "My puppy grabs stuff all day long?"

You get an A+ if you answered: "Any self-respecting puppy will grab anything interesting in his path, especially when he's bored. It is up to the people who took him from Planet Dog to create a safe environment for him here on Planet Human. That means gates and crates, careful supervision, and plenty of exercise and puppy-appropriate enrichment."

PART 6

TRAINING

27

REWARDS-BASED LEARNING

Train with Fun, Not Fear

Sometimes — often right before they get addicted to rewards-based, positive training — dog owners question its emphasis on food. They feel like they're bribing their dogs. They have a sense that their dog should just want to listen to them and obey. They want to know more about the traditional methods they remember from their childhoods, which did not involve food.

I tell them the truth: You know what's used in those methods? Fear. "If you don't do what I ask, you'll experience something bad."

If you ask me, *that's* the approach that should be raising questions in an owner's mind.

But it didn't, at first, in mine. Thirty years ago, I learned from the people I thought were experts to say "No" in a big, scary voice and to give "corrections" with a choke chain. I even used a shock collar at some point (y'know, "for my dog's own good, so he can have a bigger life"). I figured the experts knew what they were talking about, and that they must be right that a dog needed a "firm hand."

But the more dogs I lived with, and the more I observed, the more absurd that kind of approach seemed to me. It felt wrong to come down hard on my canine friends, who — I was slowly realizing — were doing their best to cope in a human environment.

So I found better experts. I learned how to teach dogs without hurting them, intimidating them, or stressing them out. Guess what? It works. It's fun. And it turns your dog into an optimistic, enthusiastic, interesting teammate rather than a robot, or a

withdrawn, hesitant student who's afraid to offer any response because it might be wrong.

As for the bribing objection, take a moment to ponder a miracle: we can reach across the great species divide and convince a
puppy to do something that's utterly unnatural for a canine — like
walking slowly at our side, with a weird-feeling trapping device
around his neck. Even more amazing is the fact that we can make
this moment feel great to him. How? By starting with the universal
gateway: food.

Food is a gift to the would-be cross-species communicator. It's
fast. It's clear. It's happy. Use food to tell your puppy, "Yes! That's
exactly what I mean!," and pretty soon your puppy ends up having
all sorts of positive feelings about you, about training, and finally
about that weird walking-by-your-side thing. Now you're on your
way to a dog who behaves beautifully according to human norms
and who also happens to be a joyful best friend. So go fill your
training pouch with yummy stuff, and let's teach your puppy how
to thrive on Planet Human.

28

THE REINFORCER

Use Your Puppy's Food Hierarchy Ladder

Folks will sometimes tell me they can't use treat-based positive reinforcement to train because their puppy "just isn't food motivated." I ask the human what exactly they've tried so far. That's when I get the blank stare. I prompt: "Fresh chicken? Cheddar cheese? Dried fish? Hot dogs?"

"Oh, wait," they say as the realization kicks in. "I can give them that stuff?"

Fantastic! We do not have a training problem. We've only just begun.

The key tool in your positive-reinforcement training arsenal is — the reinforcer! You need to put thought and effort into it. You know that one brand of shelf-stable chicken treats that you've been buying at the pet store since day 1? That's not going to do the trick when you're out on a walk and your pup hears the siren song of another dog across the street.

(For some dog-human teams, a squeaky toy or a favorite ball will be the reinforcer of choice, but for the vast majority, it's going to be food.)

The Treat Hierarchy

To set yourself up for a lifetime of focus from your dog, you need to create a pattern of being the best game in town. It's easy to earn that designation when you're in the boring old family room asking for an easy Sit. But as you progress to more difficult tasks and more distracting environments, you'll have to work your way up what I think of as the treat hierarchy ladder.

Discovering your own puppy's food hierarchy will take a bit of investigation. (Your pup will be all in for this key step in the training journey!) All dogs are not the same, and some have strong preferences. I knew a dog for whom chicken rated higher than any distraction, but turkey was meaningless. Knowing exactly what makes your dog spin her head toward you with glee comes in very handy as you train. (Plus, it's cute.)

Just to get you started, here's what's on my German Shepherd's ladder these days, roughly in order from lowest to highest:

- her own daily kibble
- a visiting dog's kibble
- typical store-bought training treats
- cheddar cheese
- sweet potato, diced into small pieces and roasted (great for pups who have sensitive stomachs)
- bits of banana, apple, sugar snap peas, and carrots. Even better if she's watched me cut it up and knows it was part of my own lunch.
- kale stems (her enthusiasm has our other dogs trying kale so very hopefully, every time, before they spit it out, confused)
- feta cheese
- hot dogs
- freeze-dried liver
- Costco cooked chicken breast
- canned cat food
- dried fish

Using the lowest-rung item you can get away with allows you to bring out the big hurrah when you really want to make an impact. I save dried fish for when I call the dogs in from barking at the foxes just beyond our fence. They zoom back, even with those interlopers out there taunting them! But if I used dried fish every day to reward Sits, soon I would not have the dried-fish tool to address the fox situation. Whatever's top rung on your dog's ladder should not be used for everyday training — and don't expect the lowest rung to allow you to compete with, say, a running deer.

Note that the context can impact treat choice. You don't want to take a can of cat food with you on a walk, but it's a perfect high-impact reward for a dog who's being calm around the new kitty in the kitchen. When you know you'll need a handful of reinforcers that are easy to deliver in a challenging environment like a busy walk — things that aren't sticky or crumbly — the store-bought treats can be best. Sometimes soft works better than crunchy, because needing to chew something can slow down the rhythm of your training. Bottom line: be ready to put in some time experimenting, and have a training bag with compartments for different items.

If you're worried that using "human food" will teach pup to beg, just don't tell pup it's human food! Begging is situational. If you feed your puppy a Milk Bone off your plate at the dinner table, you'll be teaching him to beg. It's not about the food itself.

Novelty May Be Your Dog's Favorite Food

One of my clients reported that her dog was no longer interested in training. I asked what she was using as a reinforcer. "Fresh boiled chicken." Hmm. That's a good start. Then she said, "I always use that." Aha!

Just because chicken was the most incredible taste sensation last Friday does not mean it will have the same appeal next Tuesday. While some dogs do have always-and-forever favorites, others prefer novelty. If you sense a lack of interest, try changing things up.

But Won't It Mess Up Their Diet?

People worry that using food to train will interfere with a solid diet and cause the dreaded intestinal distress. That can happen, but normally it's not an issue at all if you follow three guidelines.

1. **Use teeny, tiny pieces!** I mean minuscule, basically a whiff of the food's scent, plus a morsel that touches the tongue. You are simply creating a happy thought for the pup. Just a moment's experience of that feta cheese — "Wait, what *was* that?" — is enough for a pup to be all in with training. Keeping treats pea-sized is a good rule. If you reward your dog two dozen times in a five-minute session, that's about two tablespoons of food. Sure, if you're training a Yorkie, even that much could throw off her meal plan, but for bigger dogs it's fine.

2. **Watch the poop!** Every now and then a dog will have an unwelcome reaction to a particular item. Just remove that treat from the selection. In the meantime, use baked sweet-potato bites and boiled chicken to train with, since that's what a vet will tell you to feed a dog who has the runs.

3. **Do the shuffle!** If I'm doing a concentrated training session with a dog, I make half the treats her normal kibble, and half other yummies. The pup doesn't know which treat she'll get at any point in training, but she's eager to play the lottery because sometimes she gets her favorite. (When I take this approach, I keep the super-duper food separate from the kibble so that I can intentionally choose it when I want to.)

29

THE BASICS

How to Teach a Cue

Something beautiful happens during a puppy's introduction to official training: you can actually see the light go on when she has this empowering realization, "Hey! Life on Planet Human isn't totally unpredictable and random! I can get great stuff just by listening!"

Let's get you and your puppy to that stage as quickly as possible. While training isn't brain surgery, doing it well might not be as easy as you think. Investing a little time in refining your technique will save you (and your puppy) lots of frustration.

What to Teach When

Sometimes folks contact me saying their new puppy seems to be difficult to train. Then I show up and find that — with the best of intentions — they're "commanding" their brand-new nine-week-old pup to go "Down" and "Leave It" in a big, scary voice. Ack! Scary *and* too hard!

If you want school to go well, then start where your learner is. Once pup gets the idea that this is a fun new game where you'll be guiding her into doing things — and she gets prizes when she does them — she'll be all in.

(In this chapter, I talk about teaching *cues*. Yes, we all used to call them *commands*. But that's off-putting now that we think about it, isn't it?)

Here's my first-week list of (usually) easy-to-learn behaviors:

[Pup's name] = pup makes eye contact

Sit = pup's bum touches floor

Touch = pup's nose touches your hand (This behavior gets
     my vote for most useful cue owners haven't heard of.
     Think of it like a magnet that allows you to move your
     pup without force. Don't have a solid recall yet? Try a
     Touch in the same circumstance.)

Find It = pup searches the floor for a treat

Come = pup zooms to human

I encourage folks to spend a week getting those behaviors nice
and solid, but keeping to that short list is a challenge, since humans are always in a rush. We all want to show off a twenty-foot
"Stay" and a "Leave It" in front of a mouthwatering bone. But it's
important to try to kick your ego out of this process and focus on
connecting with your kidnapped puppy from Planet Dog. Let's
show him that it's easy for things to work out well for him here. Let
him feel like a superstar at the first five cues before moving on to the
next tier of challenges:

Spin = move around in a circle

Down = lie down

Up = move from lying down to sitting up

Through = walk under me, through my legs

Those cues can keep you both busy for a wonderful few weeks of
working together. Finally, when your puppy is really in the swing of
learning with you, you can move to the even more challenging stuff:

Stay = keep the position or spot you're in until you hear the
     release word

Wait = hang out politely (no pushing, jumping, pawing)
     until the release word

Trade = drop what's in your mouth and take what I'm offering

Leave It = ignore that item, animal, or person completely

Lure First, Then Add a Verbal Cue

Ask a seasoned trainer why one client gets much better results than
another, and they'll likely say it's the timing of feedback. Teaching
a behavior follows a certain order of operations and requires careful
timing. The folks who master that combination tend to have dogs
who seem brilliant. Whether you're teaching Sit, Down, Up, Spin,
or Through, here's the order of things. (Please don't get discour-
aged by these complicated-seeming written descriptions. Videos can
show how simple it really can be. Go to my website for a bunch of
easy-to-follow videos.)

1. **Start with no cue.** Folks always want to start by saying the
   cue word, but if you keep repeating a word that's currently
   meaningless to your puppy, she might end up associating
   it with the wrong thing. ("Oh, I guess 'Sit' must mean that
   kitty-cat who just walked by.")

2. **Use a lure.** Lure the puppy's body into position with a nug-
   get of food that you keep just in front of his nose. Think of
   it like a magnet. Move s-l-o-w-l-y so the puppy can easily
   follow. The moment the body is in the right spot, you create a marker sound (more on that below), and the treat gets
   popped in the mouth.

3. **Add the verbal cue.** Once you can reliably lure pup into
   the behavior, you can start saying the cue word as you do
   so. Now, the pup links that correct body position with the
   appropriate cue word.

4. **Change the lure to a hand signal.** Once this is all going
   swimmingly — your pup is offering that behavior four out
   of five times — you give the verbal cue as you mimic the

luring motion with an *empty* directing hand. Ideally pup performs exactly as he has been doing, and you deliver that reward just as quickly, except that it comes from the other hand. This way pup learns that following an empty hand works just as well to obtain a treat. Now you're using a hand signal.

5. **Make the hand signal smaller.** As pup catches on, the hand signal that began as a copy of the luring motion becomes smaller and smaller. Where you previously used a dramatic finger moving all the way to the ground to signify a down, you can now just flick your finger in a quick point, without moving your arm down.

6. **Drop the hand signal.** Sometimes people tell me in a very impressed tone that their brother-in-law's dog follows hand signals without him saying anything. I don't want to break the spell, so I keep it to myself that in fact that's easier. Dogs naturally pay attention to body language. Teaching them to respond to verbal cues is harder. To do that, once we have minimized the hand signal, we use timing to phase it out entirely. We say the cue, and rather than immediately giving the hand signal, we wait a second to see if pup processes what we've just asked. If not, we give that hand signal. Then we try again, with the same short delay between verbal and hand-signal cues. One of these times, your pup is going to do the thing you asked with no extra help from your body language. (Now go brag to your brother-in-law.)

The Marker: Click or "Yesss!"

If you've ever tried to learn something that feels very foreign to you, and you really had no idea whether you were getting it or not, you'll appreciate the beauty of "clicker training." You use a quick, clear sound to note the exact moment your dog got it right. The concept came from marine-mammal training, where behaviorists used whistles to tell midair dolphins, "Yes, that higher jump is exactly what we were looking for, and as soon as you swim to the side you'll get a fish." In the dog world a clicker replaced the whistle, and decades later, the Clicker Expo is the largest dog training gathering in the world. Why? Because marking works to speed learning.

Many beginning clients find using the clicker challenging, and I get it. "We need a hand for the leash, a hand for the hand signal, a hand for dispensing treats, and now a hand for the clicker?" I don't want that physical awkwardness to get in the way of training, so I start with a different but almost as effective marker: the word "Yesss!" delivered in such a way that it is very distinct, clipped, and unmistakable.

Your mission is to learn to deliver that marker with perfect timing. Do it the very second your pup's bum hits the floor in a Sit or her nose bumps your hand in a Touch. The treat always follows the marker. Soon enough, your pup will love the sound of that marker, because it's become a predictor of the reinforcer: the treat. In psych speak (learning theory), the "Yesss" has become a "conditioned reinforcer" and now carries power of its own. Now you can make your pup feel amazing the second he gets something right, because he hears that sound. In contrast, if you didn't mark that moment, you might be fumbling in your treat bag for a reward, and by the time you deliver it (the moment the pup will remember), he's no longer in that great Sit, so he's confused about what he did right.

Timing! It's worth working on. You'll need to practice. I have a trainer friend who has his clients practice clicking (or saying "Yesss!") the moment he bounces a tennis ball. You know what that teaches them? That this is harder than it looks. So practice your marker, and once you can give instantaneous feedback, watch your puppy suddenly seem like a genius.

The marker technique is especially valuable when you're teaching something new. I drop the click or the "Yesss!" once the behavior is fluent. The point of the marker is to clarify exactly what's being asked, and that kind of precision is no longer needed once the dog understands. (Keep giving the reward, though — just drop the marker.)

Distance, Duration, Distraction

To tweak whatever you're teaching, use the 3 Ds: distance, duration and distraction.

If your pup is having trouble with a cue, ponder whether you can make one of the 3 Ds easier. Did the pup ignore the treat you threw across the room when you tried "Find It"? Reduce the distance. When you asked for a "Stay," did you wait so long to release that pup gave up? Reduce the duration. Were you surprised that your pup didn't offer her usually easy "Sit" when the neighbors were over? Try again without the distraction. If you scale back at least one of your Ds, you'll likely get to a point where your pup can easily succeed and can build the skill from there.

Similarly, if you are getting a little bored and think you have nothing left to teach, you'll always find a way to make it more challenging by adjusting the 3 Ds. Get creative:

- Have you tried whispering the cue or singing it?
- What if you're lying down while you say it?
- What if you're doing jumping jacks during the Stay?

It's nice to have a dog who always Sits when you stand right in front of her in the kitchen, where you always train. But it's way more helpful for your life (not to mention more interesting and fun) if you proof that behavior by gradually varying the 3 Ds to the point that your pup will easily listen in the middle of a crowded barbecue as you call out, "Stay!" from across the yard when a guest mistakenly left a gate wide open.

Moving to Intermittent Reinforcement

One of the biggest misconceptions about positive-reinforcement, rewards-based training is that you can't ask your dog to do anything unless you have a cookie in your hand. That would be a legitimate gripe, if it were true. But it's not.

Once a pup is reliably succeeding at a certain cue, it's important to move to "intermittent reinforcement," which essentially means you no longer offer a treat every time — just often enough to keep your dog playing the lottery.

This is a critical step in training that first-timers sometimes miss. Folks get stuck in the mindset of the first week of Puppy 101, where we give treats out with abandon for every little Look, Touch, Sit, and Spin. In that earliest of phases we are seeking to create the "aha!" moment when the pup internalizes the idea that listening for a cue and responding with a behavior is the surest way to get stuff that makes them happy — a treat at this stage, and later on the throwing of a ball or opening of a gate.

Once that light bulb has gone on, it's time to move on to the next big idea, which is essentially the lottery concept: you gotta play to win! We want to build into our pups the understanding that not every cue is rewarded with a treat, but just because they didn't get rewarded for one particular Down, it doesn't mean the whole system is defunct. It just means she has to keep trying, and one of these times there will be a reward. Shifting to intermittent rewards builds resilience and turns your pup into one who will keep trying.

The easiest way into this transition is to start asking for twofers and threefers: two or three behaviors in sequence. A puppy in her first training class gets a click and a treat for a Sit, and right after that a click and a treat for a Touch. A week later, when the pup is reliably performing both of those cues in class, we move into a twofer: we ask for a Sit and immediately after that ask for a Touch. The pup gets a click and a treat after the second behavior, or after the third in a Touch-Spin-Sit threefer.

"Ack!" you're thinking! "No click after that first behavior? Will my pup think she's suddenly doing it wrong?" I promise, if you group those cues together closely enough, your pup won't have time to be disturbed about that. However, this is where a new sound, an informative marker, could come in handy. You can use a quick "Good" or "Mm-hmm" after the first behavior. It doesn't promise a treat, but it confirms your pup did something right.

Moving to intermittent reinforcement has the counterintuitive effect of making dogs more focused, rather than less. When the treats aren't automatic, the learner will try a little harder, with more intense eye contact, a straighter sit, a quicker down. He'll essentially say, "Huh. No treat? Watch this!"

You'll quickly be able to move to intermittent rewards for the cues that are easiest for your pup. But for one you're struggling with — say, "Down" — pup still gets a click and a treat every single time those elbows hit the ground. Clear, consistent reinforcement builds a behavior. Once it's easy for your pup, there's no longer a need to provide that bright neon sign.

When Can I Drop the Rewards Altogether?

There is, inevitably, this question: "So when can we stop with the treats altogether?" (Dear reader, I know you are not the one with the cold, hard heart that puts forth this query, but you'll need to know how to answer those who might ask it.) It is, in a certain sense, a logical question. After all, if we're scaling back to intermittent reinforcement, it seems we're heading in the direction of none at all.

Ah, but we're not.

We are often asking dogs to do things for *our* convenience that:

- they would not do on their own
- are not intrinsically rewarding to them
- are even in opposition to their own natural instincts and desires

The science of learning theory says that none of us does anything for very long unless it is somehow reinforcing, rewarding, or clearly in our own best interest. Despite Lassie and the mountains of self-sacrificing-dog myth in the back of our collective mind, that is true for dogs as well.

For me, a promise of a little morsel of food every now and then is not too much to ask to get our dogs — the puppies we've kidnapped from their own culture — to *want* to do the weird stuff that's prized in our culture.

So there's never a day when we stop rewarding. As time goes on, you'll find that it becomes second nature to incorporate powerful "real-life rewards" into your daily routine with your dog. (The nice Sit earns an open car door and a promise of adventure, rather than a cookie.) Those, along with warm praise, may become your primary way of rewarding your dog when he has learned the basics. But do the food rewards ever come to an end? Not for me. And honestly, as my dear old dogs have aged and moved onto the heavenly branch of our pack, I'm happy for every sweet moment when I gave them a dried liver cube just for that cute little Spin they learned a dozen years ago.

30

YOUR TRAINING VIBE

Posture, Tone, and Mindset Matter

Quick: who was your favorite teacher? Chances are it was somebody charismatic and warm, who had a confidence that made you want to play along. If you want your puppy to learn fast, focus on the attitude you're projecting. What can you do with your voice and your body language to create a great learning environment?

If you've ever watched a trainer get an amazing response out of your dog three minutes after they've met — when you feel like you've been trying the exact same thing with zero results — this is likely a big part of what's happening. The trainer has a wonderful teaching vibe, and you can learn that too.

Inviting Tone of Voice

At my first-ever dog training class, I watched the instructor bellow "Come!" to my puppy in a do-it-or-else voice. My usually exuberant pup held back, then crept toward him very slowly. I was just twelve, but even then I knew it felt wrong.

Fifty years later, I sound like a cartoon character as I call dogs in a high, cheery tone. It is a sound that promises good things, not a sound that threatens.

Even though dog training has come a long way, people often instinctively boom "Come!," "Leave it!," or "Down!" in a stern, intimidating voice. That may seem effective (especially to somebody who doesn't notice the dog's hesitant or fearful body language), but dogs are sensitive to tone, and in the end this pup will link his owner and training with the feeling of "Uh-oh." That makes him less eager to engage and less likely to offer the behaviors you're hoping to see. Training tends to dwindle off because nobody's having fun.

It's so easy to do it differently! Just keep that voice light. We're going for the voice of a teacher, not a drill sergeant. It should be strong and clear — no mumbling, no confusion — but inviting.

Clear Body Language

When your puppy is trying to figure out what you're asking for, his first stop is going to be your body language. That's the most fundamental way dogs communicate with each other. Getting your body working for you — rather than against you — will turbocharge your training success.

When people are new to training, their body language usually telegraphs uncertainty. They slouch, they look around, they fumble. Not sure what you look like? Prop your phone up to record a few minutes of your training session. If you're like the rest of us — even people who train for a living — you'll see room for improvement.

Here's how. First, take a deep breath and think through what you're about to ask of your dog. Have a plan. What's the verbal cue? What's the hand signal? When will you mark and reward? If you and pup aren't successful on the first try, how will you decrease one of the 3 Ds (distance, duration, or distractions) to create a win? The twenty seconds it takes to ponder these questions ahead of time will show up in how you hold yourself and give direction, making learning much easier for your dog.

In addition to conveying general confidence, you want your body to be in sync with the specific "ask" you're making.

- If you're teaching a beginning recall ("Come!") but you're standing stock still, you're sending a mixed message. To a dog, that tall, immobile posture is the opposite of inviting. Think about this: what do dogs do when they want another dog to run toward them? They get low, wiggle some, wag around, and maybe start running themselves. Mimic that body language, and watch your dog happily figure out exactly what "Come" means.

- Conversely, if you're having trouble teaching Stay, check your own body. If you're slouchy or moving, you're sending a confusing message. You can often hold a dog in a Stay just by keeping your body utterly still, leaning forward a bit, and maintaining eye contact.

- When attempting to encourage their puppy to move forward on leash, I see people standing up straight and pulling the leash. That stance is working against them. Use your inviting body, with zero leash pressure, to get your pup going. Bend your knees, get your face closer to the pup, and do some quick dancing steps to engage him. "Let's walk!"

Whatever you're trying to teach your dog, remember that it's largely your body that's going to teach it at first. What can you do with the way you're holding yourself and moving that will make it clearer to your dog what you're looking for?

Stress-Free Attitude

Now that you've got your voice and your body working for you, it's time to get your emotions on board. Do a quick gut check before you pick up a leash: are you in a good emotional place? If you've had a bad day at work or an unsettling conversation with your mother-in-law, can you readjust? If you're still feeling off, don't train with your dog. That stress is going to go straight into your session, and it'll set you back.

Even if you're feeling fine at the start of training, frustration can soon set in if you don't guard against it. Maybe two days ago you'd worked up to a one-minute, ten-foot Stay, and today your dog is acting like she's never heard that word. The worst thing you can do is to get cranky and insist on making that Stay happen just like it did before. Instead, take a deep breath and laugh it off, then go back to something that's an easy win — maybe a string of Touches, Spins, and Sits. If you're ready to tackle Stay again, then start at the easiest level possible: Step back two feet and immediately return. She did it! Ta-da! Now build slowly from there.

For you and your puppy to grow as a happy, in-sync team, the key is to delight in small victories. If you do that, training will keep feeling light and fun for you both. And if that happens, you'll opt to train again tomorrow and the next day. You know what that means? That reliable long Stay really will be right around the corner.

31

YOUR CUES

When Puppy "Doesn't Listen"

If you're frustrated that your pup "doesn't listen," I urge you to consider what she is actually hearing each day. Take a minute to examine precisely what you've been asking for and how you've been asking for it. You may well find that your puppy's listening skills are not the issue.

Anyone who's tried to pick up a foreign language knows the frustration of hearing the same word used in different ways. "Wait, I thought I knew what that meant, but now I'm not sure." Sometimes, just as you think you know what to call something, you hear it called something else. "Ugh, never mind. I thought I was getting good at this, but I give up."

Alas, as we humans try to teach puppies our language, we confuse them in just this way, slowing their learning. Sometimes it's because the various people in the puppy's life use different cues, and sometimes it's because we haven't thought through what a particular cue really means. Either issue can result in a pup disengaging from the learning process because it feels like an unwinnable game.

Down or Off?

Here's a quiz: Which spouse is using the cue "Down" correctly?

1. The husband walks into the kitchen, sees the dog counter surfing, and says, "Down!"

2. The wife is walking the dog when a toddler approaches. She says, "Down!" so that the dog will lie at the child's feet for easier petting.

This, of course, is a trick question. They are both wrong — because they're not on the same page about what their cues mean. As a result, their poor puppy is set up for confusion. If you want your dog to have a solid response to "Down," it can't mean both "Remove yourself from that higher-level area" *and* "Lie on the floor." Pick one meaning and find another word for the other behavior. (The cue to stop counter surfing could be "Off," or the request to lie down could be "Lay.")

Use the Exact Same Words

The low-hanging fruit of solving this problem is to get everyone in your pup's orbit using identical verbal cues. Many frustrated puppies are forced to try to learn from different family members using the following cues interchangeably:

- "Sit" or "Sit Down"
- "Down" or "Lay" or "Lay Down" or "Lie Down"
- "Off" or "Down"
- "Stay" or "Wait"
- "Come" or "Here"

It doesn't matter *which* you choose; it matters *that* you choose. So have a household meeting (or a meeting with your inconsistent self), and decide once and for all what to call these behaviors. Then post that list on the fridge as a reminder.

Create Distinct Hand Signals

I ask my clients to send me one-minute videos of their training at home a few days after our lesson. There's so much to think about — the verbal cue, the hand signal, body position, marker timing, treat delivery — that it's easy to make small but significant mistakes. Each day of slightly messed-up practice makes things worse. This week, I had to laugh because one of my favorite clients was asking her puppy to Touch — while making the hand signal she uses for Stay. Talk about a puppy dilemma!

We could debate exactly which hand signals are best for different cues, but it comes down to personal choice. What matters most is that you think through what your hands are saying. Your pup is absolutely watching — body language is a more natural communication style for our dogs than our verbal cues — so be utterly clear and intentional with those motions. And then have the whole household rehearse them together.

Just for fun, if you have kids, play a game where one person gives the signals and the other humans offer the behavior you think was asked for. You'll all learn quickly how important precision is.

Stay vs. Place vs. Wait

Think you know exactly what Sit means? It's not as simple as it sounds. Some teach that a Sit means the dog's bum touches the ground. Others teach that Sit means maintaining that position until released with an "Okay." My definitions don't have to be the same as yours — I could decide "Banana" means "Go into your crate" — but we all have to be consistent every single time we work with our own dogs.

That's harder than it sounds. Perhaps the best example of potential confusion comes with the family of cues that involve limiting movement: Stay, Wait, and Place. Here are my own usages:

- **Stay.** When I cue Stay, it's like we're playing that old tag game: "Freeze!" Pup should not move: no shifting between a Sit and a Down, and no inching forward. The pup can swivel her head to watch me, but that's about it.

- **Place.** When I ask a dog to go to her Place, she goes to a clearly defined space (like a mat). She can shift positions and move around as much as she wants as long as she stays in that space. She can inch forward to the edge of that space but not step out of it.

- **Wait.** My use of Wait seems complicated, but dogs get it 100 percent. Essentially, it's this: "You're going to get that thing you want, but you need to hang out calmly for just a sec first until you get my signal." The circumstances (and the thing they want) vary quite a lot. I might mean that I don't want them jumping into the car yet, or going through the gate yet, or eating their food yet, or grabbing the toy yet. With Wait, I don't care what position they're in, and they can move around. But until I say, "Okay!" they can't go for that one thing we both know they're thinking about. When I write it out like that, it seems nuts, but the proof is in the behavior: the dogs get it.

These three cues illustrate that close but not identical behaviors require different cues. If you're using these terms interchangeably, or using just one of these cues but with different meanings in different circumstances, that explains why your pup's response is not yet rock-solid.

It sounds over-the-top nerdy, but truly: take the time to write out your cues and think through what they actually mean. Discuss with the household. Then give your pup that nice clear direction, and reward accordingly. You may feel stunned — and a little guilty — when your dog suddenly seems so much smarter.

32

TRICK TRAINING

Spin Your Way to Happy Learning

Your puppy has neither a laptop nor a cell phone. While the whole world is coming at you through those screens, your dog just has… you. And if the only thing you can think of to pass the time together is a walk, well, that leaves a lot of hours in the day when your puppy needs to dream up some other activities. Let's see, maybe chewing the chair leg? Barking at bikers? Getting the zoomies during your Zoom call?

Having an expanded repertoire of interesting things to do with your puppy is one secret to a much more rewarding relationship and a surprisingly better-behaved dog.

Bonding through Play

Think about the last time you played a game with your family. Whether it was Pictionary, Scrabble, or charades, I bet there was laughter, and you all felt closer afterward.

Now ponder that same dynamic with your dog. Consider playing "bored games" with your puppy just the way you play board games with your family.

Long ago, it didn't occur to me to do much beyond the usual things with our dogs: big walks, training with cues like Sit, Down, and Stay, cuddling, and maybe a little game of Tug. I didn't teach tricks — like Spin, Roll Over, or Through — because I didn't see the point.

In contrast, it was obvious to me that all the time we spent playing games with our young daughters was well spent, because:

- it gave us something to do together;
- it built their brains and increased their confidence; and
- it was fun, so it added another positive layer to our relationship.

I wish my old self had realized that every one of those upsides also applies to playing interesting games with your dog.

Brain Games

So, what kinds of games are we talking about playing with our pups? Of course, it's great to have the classics like Fetch and Tug in the mix. But what about some activities that are heavier on mental stimulation?

Too often, people don't think of training as a fun thing for their puppy to do. Quite likely that's because it's not fun for the human involved. Why? Because they're inside their own head, where dog training is linked to stress. "I need to get Rufus to Heel right now because my neighbors see how out of control he is, and I'm embarrassed." (A quick digression: can we all just give each other a break on the dog judginess? People on Nextdoor.com, I'm talking to you.)

Done right — with positive reinforcement — training is fun. It's the doggy equivalent of a board game.

Developing a "Tricks" Mindset

To get an owner into a playful headspace, I start with Spin instead of something "useful" like Sit, Down, or Stay. Immediately, the vibe in the room is better for learning. The human is no longer obsessed with the result — who cares if the puppy can Spin? — but is now curious, amused, and eager to try.

Here's what happens next: The puppy learns Spin in about a minute. The puppy's enthusiastic response cracks the owner up, so she starts asking for Spins all week at home. There's a Spin before food, a Spin before getting up on the couch, and a Spin to show off in front of the neighbors. The kids think it's awesome and have started to do it too. The puppy is all in and suddenly seems smarter to everyone.

They are laughing. They feel closer.

Look at that. The magic of games happens with dogs, too.

All Training Is Tricks!

The next big mental leap is realizing that to your puppy, training is all Spin! Your puppy has no idea that some behaviors are "useful" and some are not. To him they're all just words that can mean a chance to earn chicken: "Yay! Fun. Love to play this with my people."

Training this way is an engaging, enriching game you can weave throughout a day with your otherwise-bored dog. If you need to teach yourself that training can be lighthearted, start with Spin, and crack yourself up. Then move onto Touch and Through (passing through your legs). Now that you have the hang of a more relaxed mindset, you can throw in Down and Stay.

Be ready, because after two weeks of throwing this into every day, your puppy is going to change. She's going to look at you differently. There is going to be a brightness and a focus you never saw before. She's going to gaze at you, ready to listen. Just FYI.

Once you're all in the swing of this kind of play, you can link cues together for a performance: start with a Sit, then a Through, followed by a nice Down-Stay, then an exuberant Come, and a big double Spin finish! Have a race to see which family member can complete this little dance with the dog fastest.

So, after reading this, how's your mindset? If you're feeling overwhelmed, I encourage you back to Spin. Just Spin. Give it a try, and see where it leads. No pressure. It's just a game.

33

EVERYDAY PRACTICE

Find the Time in Routine Moments

Feel like you don't have time to train with your puppy? Yes, you do! You can build learning into your day in tiny increments that make it seem like it takes no time at all. Just use your household routine to prompt a handful of one-minute sessions throughout the day. It'll hardly feel like you're doing much, but a month later, you will have an amazing relationship with your puppy, an addictive new hobby, and some unexpected moments of delight in your house.

The Secret of Daily Reinforcement

Want to know why this approach works so well? The answer is in Sit. Everybody's dog knocks it out of the park when it comes to Sit. Unfortunately, for many dogs, that's about it. Down is a blank stare. Stay is anything but. And as for lying calmly on a mat while some-body's cooking? Forget it.

Why, then, is Sit always a solid skill? Because it's the one cue that all owners work into their daily routine. Every single time they feed the dog, they ask for a Sit first. The dog Sits; the dog gets a reward. Reinforcement 365 days a year builds a rock-solid behavior.

Daily training like this in moments beyond the food bowl gives you a chance to naturally apply that same approach with a host of other cues. Read on to see how to link the things you do every day to cues you can practice and reward. And then, a month from now, re-port back about how attentively your puppy is gazing at you, and how you're cracking up while you text videos of her tricks to your mom.

Cup of Coffee and "Down"

Let's say you work from home and pour yourself a cup of coffee several times a day. How many times does your puppy pad after you, ever hopeful? Turn that pattern into an easy training win. Keep a cute ceramic container of your dog's kibble on the counter. Every time you go into the kitchen to fill your mug, lure your pup into the Down position with a piece of kibble. In a week, your pup will be throwing a fabulous Down every time you venture near that pot, which will make you laugh and exclaim with glee, "Who's my goodest boy?" Now the Down is just as strong as the Sit, and you're on your way.

Breakfast and "Wait"

Your dog already does the nice Sit before the dog bowl. How about adding a Wait cue? When your pup is sitting, and you're holding the bowl, you say, "Wait," and pause for just a second or two while pup holds that Sit. Then you put the bowl down. If she moves for the bowl before you've put it on the floor, raise it again. Try again. Once she retains that Sit until the bowl gets to the floor, release her to eat with an "Okay!" (Don't expect a long wait right at the beginning. Keep it to a second or two at first so that you're setting pup up for success.)

After a week of taking just seconds to focus on this each day, you will have taught an incredibly helpful cue to your dog. Now you can take that Wait out for a test drive. Every day will hand you a dozen opportunities to ask for a Wait. Practice it when pup is about to barge out the door, shove through the gate, launch into the car, or leap onto the couch. Pup still gets access to those things, but now they come through listening to you.

I bet you can predict what happens after a month of that unofficial-seeming training: you can add Wait to the "solid" column.

Dinner and Tricks

When serving pup's dinner, you could also practice the Sit and Wait — or you could use that time to teach and practice something else. How about asking for a Shake or a Spin before the bowl goes down? How about eventually developing a little routine — perhaps a Spin-Sit-Shake-Down-Wait?

The result? Daily smiles for the entire family, plus a nice household mood boost. Somehow this pup just gets cuter and cuter!

Screen Time and "Come"

Any chance someone in the family is spending way too much time in front of screens? How about breaking it up by playing a fun, raucous game — outside, if you can — every night after dinner for ten minutes? Load everyone up with yummy pup treats cut into tiny pieces. Get into a big circle and call your pup back and forth between you. She gets one delicious nibble whenever she runs to the person who just called her. So simple, so effective.

Most owners don't practice the recall cue ("Come" or "Here"), but they sure try to use it! They use it to call their pup *away* from all the fun stuff — the dog park, the neighbor's yard, the deer they're chasing. All that does is make that cue into the thing your dog is sure to ignore.

If you take ten minutes to play this little game every night, using super-happy voices, lots of cheer, and always the very best treats, suddenly that word is going to perk up your pup's ears when it counts. It just might save her life one day.

Zoom Calls and "Place"

It's like clockwork: the second the Zoom meeting starts, the puppy is pawing at your elbow. You push her away, and she jumps up on your thigh. Your colleagues were amused when this was new. It is no longer new.

This is a golden opportunity to teach Place. Put a mat near your desk. The first day, every time you happen to see your pup go near that mat, toss a piece of her kibble onto it. She will start hanging out near the mat more. Once she does, toss the kibble only when she actually steps on the mat, then only when she stands completely on the mat, and finally only when she lies on the mat. Once she's regularly doing that, call it "Place."

Eventually, when you start a Zoom call and she paws at you, you can say, "Place," and she'll know that the most rewarding spot she can be in at that moment is her mat. Want to make that behavior rock-solid? Put another mat in the kitchen. Practice Place every time you cook or sit down to eat a meal.

Bathroom and "Stay"

Does your puppy follow you everywhere? It's okay, you can admit it: you always have company when you go to the bathroom. Let's turn that into some multitasking. If your pup is at the early stages of learning Stay, meaning you can step just a foot away for a moment, bathroom visits offer a perfect opportunity to turn that into a Stay you can ask for when the relatives are unloading the food for Thanksgiving and the front door is wide open.

Once again, prep by keeping a cute little ceramic jar of treats on the counter. As you approach the bathroom door, turn around and ask your puppy for a Down. Reward with a treat, and ask for a Stay. Step a foot into the bathroom, then come right back and reward. Repeat a dozen times over the next few days until pup has the hang of lying in a Stay at the threshold to the bathroom.

Now you're ready to use the cue for real. Have to use the bathroom? "Stay." Pup now knows that this moment is a chance to get a treat just by lying quietly at the door.

Once pup can manage a solid indoor Stay, you'll be ready to make the most of the everyday walk to the mailbox. Clip a long line to your pup's collar, and ask her to Stay in a Down on your front step. Then take a few steps out toward the mailbox and come right back and treat. Then do it again, and go a bit farther. Repeat until you can go all the way to the mailbox and back, giving pup a great treat each time she keeps that Stay until your return.

See how this is *way* more fun, for both you and the puppy, than shoving the door shut in her face and trudging out to the mailbox? Just another example of how dog training offers a path to happiness!

Training as a Way of Life

Most people vaguely think they might train with their dogs if only they had the time. But how much time does it take to ask for that Sit before the food bowl? Right — about one second. With a tiny bit of prep and intention — but very little time — you'll discover that you and your puppy can do amazing things together. I know you're already bonded, but just wait. There's even more ahead for you both.

PULLING ON LEASH

Move Your Dog with Your Brain, Not Your Brawn

One of the most common requests humans bring to dog trainers is "Can you just stop him from pulling so much on the leash?"

The funny thing is, if dogs could hire human trainers, here's what they'd say: "Can you just stop him from pulling so much on the leash?" They might even add, "Come to think of it, can you just stop him from constantly manhandling my body, when a simple, polite request would do?"

If your puppy frequently uses his body to get what he wants — by knocking into you, pawing at you, jumping on you, or pulling on leash — I beg you to take just one day to notice that this dynamic works both ways. Pay attention to just how many times you use your superior strength instead of using your intelligence and knowledge about training to get your puppy to do what you'd like. How often do you tug, yank, pull, push, or lift your dog, perhaps using his leash as a steering wheel or his collar or harness as a handle?

Folks, your dogs are learning this world's rules from you.

There's a better way. Instead of relying on physical force, employ that big brain of yours. How many times today can you resist the quick and easy way of getting your puppy where you want him, and instead begin creating a collaborative dynamic that serves you both beautifully? Challenge yourself to use your voice, your body language, your treats, and your bond with your pup instead of using the leash or your hands.

Give a Heads-Up

Pro tip: start by using your words.

Let's say, on your walk, you've stopped to chat with a friend or to wait for the signal to cross the street. Your puppy has been waiting patiently, sitting politely or standing quietly, perhaps watching some kids down the street, when suddenly you're done with the conversation or the crossing indicator turns green, and you yank him out of his reverie.

What does that sudden tug teach your pup? First, it drives home the point that weird and sudden leash pressure is a way of life, so now it won't feel strange to him when he creates that pressure himself by pulling or dashing. Second, it teaches him to be on guard for one of those yanks, to never fully relax on a walk with you. That makes your walks open season for pull-and-yank, plus a bit of anxiety. I'll argue that's not a small thing.

It's so easy to do better. Simply give your dog a heads-up, an invitation, before moving off. That's all! Before taking a step, just cue your dog: "Okay, Spot, let's go!" You could also pat your thigh or make a clicking or kissing noise — any kind of communication that loops your dog into the plan.

It may seem minuscule, this change, but when you watch it in action, you suddenly see a team. It's huge.

Use Your Brain to Move Your Dog

Just today one of my favorite clients mentioned that her dog gets testy whenever her collar is grabbed. My question: Why are you grabbing her collar so much?

As simple as it feels to us to snag our dogs by that omnipresent handle, in the long run it interferes with the behavior and the relationship we want. Try using your brain to move your puppy, not your muscles.

- Want your dog to get off the couch? Don't grab his collar; just stick out your hand and say, "Touch." (You've taught this, right? The easiest cue of all time? Pup's nose touches your outstretched hand. You'll find a thousand uses.)

- Want your dog to hold still so you can put on the leash? Don't grab his collar, ask for a Sit.

- Want to interrupt your dog's chase of the cat? Don't grab his collar, just scoot in the opposite direction with a toy and call him in a crazy-happy tone of voice. Reward him when he comes to you.

The collar grab, like the leash yank, is the instinctive way we humans get control. It's easy to fall into the habit of using this kind of low-level physical force all day long. If you don't think about it very much, it just seems normal.

But the more you *do* think about it, the stranger it seems that we casually and frequently use our superior physical strength (or the control we can get with various tools) to force our best friends — these sentient, intelligent souls who are fully capable of learning the most intricate behaviors — to put their bodies exactly where we want them. Some dogs accept this constant contact with resignation, but many others mentally tune out when they can't seem to escape these unpleasant physical intrusions. Some may come to rely on the barrage of yanks, pushes, and pulls for direction. A few start to growl or show other signs of defensive aggression in order to stop the assaults.

Remember, in every interaction we have with our dogs, we are teaching them who we are. Ponder what vibe you want to express. Personally, I want to have a friendly, fun, trusting, and respectful relationship with my dogs — and I see plenty of evidence that makes me believe that they want that, too.

Challenge Yourself

Years ago, in one of the most fun dog training classes I've been to, the instructor had us all tie a loose knot — maybe four inches in diameter — in the middle of our leashes. Then we spent ten minutes walking around the facility in a line, passing each other again and again. The winner was the dog-human pair who had the loosest knot after all of that.

To accomplish this, we used happy voices, kissy noises, and dancing steps. There was cheese and chicken, along with a robust history of positive reinforcement. We made the most of cues like Touch and Look and Heel and Side (a sit at the left side, both of you facing forward). It was a blast, because it showed us how far we had come from the days when we too thought it was normal to just pull our dogs around. It was a reflection of how much more rewarding and cooperative our relationships with our dogs had become.

Give it a try. Watch what happens when you start communicating with your dog rather than using your superior strength to go places and do things with him. I think you'll find that your time with your dog quickly becomes less of a struggle and more enjoyable, as it should be when you experience life in sync with a respected friend.

How loose is your knot?

35

GROUP TRAINING CLASS

Five Survival Tips

If you've just emerged from your first-ever group training class, you have my sympathies. For the unprepared, that experience can be a rude awakening.

Whether your pup is pulling wildly toward the other puppies, acting like she's never met you, barking while the instructor talks, or hiding under your chair, it feels like a nightmare. You might be tempted to tell people this is actually your neighbor's dog and you're just pitching in.

After that kind of introduction, many dog owners listen to the little voice in their head whispering, "Let's just forget we paid for all six lessons and call it a day." That's a shame, because when humans stick with it, they often walk out of the final class amazed at the turnaround they've experienced.

To help you get to that magic day, the best programs have a surprising rule for the first day of class: no dogs allowed. During that key first session, blissfully free of doggy distractions, the instructors set the humans up for success. They set appropriate expectations and give some make-or-break tips on how to manage your puppy during class.

If your upcoming class doesn't offer that dog-free first class, make yourself a nice cup of tea, sit down in your quiet kitchen, and absorb these five survival tips before you head into the joyful chaos that is Puppy 101.

Bring Your Sense of Humor and Reasonable Expectations

Sometimes the secret to life is low expectations, and that is dramatically true here. Assume the first class or two will feel ridiculously hard. Be thrilled if *anything* goes right! This mindset is key, because the more stress you bring into that training area, the more your puppy will feel it. Take a deep breath, and hold on to your sense of humor.

Keep in mind that this is a class, not a competition. If your puppy is the most disruptive in the class, don't shrink in embarrassment. Instead, find the warmest fellow student so you can share a smile about it. Then remember that this means you have the greatest potential for the "most improved" award after six weeks!

Use Amazing Treats

The same puppy who Sits and Stays beautifully for you in your kitchen may act as if he does not even hear you in class. With the cascade of new distractions — a different space, other puppies, and new people — you're going to need help pulling his attention back to you. Put serious thought and prep into surprising your new student with fabulous taste sensations in class, linking the first group training experience with dried fish, liver, cheddar cheese, or fresh chicken.

Bring more food than you think you'll need. First-time students always run out! You'll be asking your puppy for many behaviors, and you need to be ready to reward. You'll be using tiny pieces (the size of a pea), but it adds up. This all means you need an official treat pouch. A baggy in your pocket is going to be way too clumsy to work with.

Start in the Parking Lot

So, you're going to drive up to class with a terrific treat pouch ready to go. The next little secret is to let your pup in on this news the minute you get out of the car. Wave that tiny piece of ham past his nose and ask for a quick Sit. Reward. Your newly focused-on-you pup thinks, "Wow! What is happening?" As you walk in, ask for a behavior that is solid at home — perhaps just a series of easy Touches. As your pup revels in her ability to snag a great new treat just by listening a bit, you're walking successfully past the dogs and people who might otherwise have been a crazy distraction.

Do that every time you come to class, and soon you've built a pattern. You're the most reliably rewarding thing in your dog's life, even when you're out and about. Get ready for some very nice attention to follow.

Expect to Miss Some Instruction

During class, you will probably need to work hard just managing your pup. Don't worry if that means you miss some of what's being said. It may help to present your pup with a new chew, like a bully stick, so that you can listen to the instructor as she explains the next exercise. If your pup is slightly more advanced, you can quietly ask for (and reward!) Sits, Touches, and eye contact while the trainer is talking.

"Wait, how am I supposed to listen if I'm busy with toys and management?" I hear ya. It is frustrating, indeed. But even if you have to work so hard on managing your wild creature that you barely absorb the official instruction, this experience can be a fantastic hour for your pup. You're out of the house, and pup is seeing the world. If you can stay cool and positive, this is bonding time for the two of you. Next time, it'll be easier, and the time after that even more so. Just keep your head in the right place, and keep on coming to class. (The exception to the "keep on coming" advice is regarding the pup hiding under the chair. That's fine at first, but after 10 minutes or so we want to see her getting curious, venturing out, feeling safe.)

Do Your Homework

While we humans are working our bums off during class, our dogs are maybe, sort of, halfway learning a cue or two. What's *really* happening is that humans are learning how to teach various behaviors effectively. It's the at-home practice that results in your dog truly learning the cues.

Carve out a few minutes a day to practice exactly what you did in class. Start in the kitchen, progress to the yard, then take the big step to the distraction-filled street. Be ready to be amazed at (1) how much your dog adores this time with you, and (2) how incredibly smart he is.

One of the best ways to make your at-home training more effective is to ask somebody else to take a few quick videos of you working together. (Or just prop your phone up at the right angle and record.) Take it from me, even dog trainers catch themselves screwing up when they see themselves on video. Look closely, find that misstep, shift your approach, and watch how the results change. Noticing tiny improvements each week can be addictive.

I'm a big fan of a well-run group class, and here's why:

- Those distractions that are so challenging at first end up teaching your dog to focus in any environment.

- You learn from watching other teams work together.

- You gain perspective when you see everybody else's strengths and weaknesses.

- Both you and your puppy make friends — which can start with funny commiseration, and build into great playdates, joint walks, and even pet-sitting trades.

Yet another bonus to group class: you'll have eyewitnesses to cheer the fact that you've really come a long way from that first crazy day!

PART 7

BEING A
GREAT OWNER

PART 7

BEING A
GREAT OWNER

36

QUALITY OF LIFE

Five Common Mistakes

If there were something simple you could do that would make your dog much happier, you'd do it in a flash, right?

Every day I see owners going to great lengths, and spending small fortunes, to improve their dogs' lives. That's why I'm perplexed when I see those very same folks ignoring the smaller, easy-to-rectify issues that are diminishing their dog's daily quality of life, causing anything from mild irritation to major pain.

Maybe this happens because marketers are eager to direct owners' attention to expensive food and treats, beds and toys, training tools, dog walkers and doggy daycare. But some of the most important ways to support our canine friends are low-ticket items that nobody is advertising. Here are five key things to keep top of mind.

Long Nails

Ready for the hard truth? You need to trim your dog's nails every few weeks.

I know. Your dog hates it. You hate it. So you put it off and ask the vet or groomer to do it whenever your dog goes in. Unfortunately, unless you're in the habit of monthly visits, that's not nearly often enough.

Here's why too-long nails can make your dog feel miserable and affect his long-term health:

- Each step your dog takes on those nails puts inappropriate pressure on the toes. That hurts, and sometimes it makes those toes twist unnaturally.

- The pain from those steps causes dogs to compensate by adjusting their posture. That can cause orthopedic issues and lead to hind-end weakness and soreness.

- Long nails give dogs even less grip on slippery wood or tile floors, increasing the likelihood of muscle strain. This is particularly hard on older dogs who've lost muscle tone. It's terrible to feel insecure walking across the kitchen.

With a few exceptions, if a dog's nails are clicking on the floor, it's time to trim. And if you're thinking that clipping them short enough to eliminate that click would mean cutting the quick, I have more bad news for you. The quick — the nerve inside the nail that bleeds if you cut it — grows along with the nail. So if you let the nails get too long, the quick gets too long, too. The only remedy is an intense phase of even more frequent trimming! The quick always recedes from the edge of the nail. After six weeks of frequent, careful trimming, the quick should be short enough to let you clip the nails enough to stop them clicking on the floor.

Maybe you've always known how important nail trimming is, but you want to leave it to the "experts" because you still remember that time you made Rover bleed. My own "aha!" moment came when my daughter interned at the local vet and let me know that there is no perfect nail magic happening in that back room. They do their best, but sometimes they mess up, too. The difference is that you don't see it happen, and they use styptic to stop the bleeding.

That information was eye-opening to me. I realized I was putting my dogs through extra stress just so that I could avoid the drama myself. I decided that if this is to be done every three weeks, it's better for my dogs to experience it with me, in the comfort of their own home. So I worked on this skill. There are plenty of good guides online. It is not brain surgery. I'm pretty good at it now, and you can be, too. Here's what'll help:

- Pick your time. A super-tired dog is best. Possibly even more important: a nonstressed you.

- Make sure your clippers are sharp. Dull blades cause compression, and so they hurt. I buy new clippers fairly regularly, since I clip a lot of dogs.

- Try a grinder instead of a clipper. I have come to adore this option, which leaves the nails with nice soft edges and entirely avoids the possibility of cutting the quick. However, grinders take longer and make a noise. I find dogs have preferences between clippers and grinders, so I let them take the lead.

- Take the time to condition your dog to the experience. Pair the sight of the clippers or the sound of the grinder with something delicious. Dried fish! Feta cheese! Do that as frequently as you must until you see that head swivel eagerly at the sight of the tool. Next step: touch the tool to the paw, then treat. Baby steps can work wonders. (Although this may sound like it takes tons of time and patience, each little interaction takes only seconds.)

- Remember there's no rule that you have to do all the nails at once. With some dogs I do two and call it a day.

I implore you to work on this. You'll screw up at first, and you'll want to give up. Stick with it, because the more you do it, the better you get. And once you're skilled, you're going to hit that every-three-weeks mark. It may never be your favorite part of the day, but you and your dog can get to the point where you don't dread it. The sooner you can get brave and learn to deal with this, the sooner your dog will be walking more comfortably.

Clinking Tags

Does the sound of your dog's clinking tags ever bug you? Now imagine those tags were around your own neck 24/7, and you had incredibly acute hearing. Sad, right?

Sure, maybe most dogs get used to it. But why in the world should they have to? These days there are fantastic products out there that make loudly clinking tags a torture device of the past.

Before you examine those new options, take the easiest step: simply reduce the number of jingling objects. Remove outdated tags and ponder whether you really need that rabies tag. (Many counties do not require them, as the license itself is proof of current vaccination.)

Once you've minimized the number of tags, you can bundle the remaining ones so that they don't make noise knocking against each other. Plenty of do-it-yourselfers use rubber bands or electrical tape. However, if you're looking for a cuter option, there are now great little pouches that can slip on and hold those tags together in silence.

Alternatively, you can opt for a rubber ID tag rather than a metal one, or buy rubber silencers that fit around the edges of the tags. Available online, they come in all sorts of colors and in the typical tag shapes.

Finally, there are slide-on tags that loop over the collar and lie flat. (I use these, with our family contact information, for my foster dogs, because I can easily move them from collar to collar.) You can also order a custom collar with ID information engraved either on the buckle or on the collar itself. (Is it possible that someone who finds your dog would somehow miss the ID information if it's not in the traditional dangling tag? Or find it hard to read if your dog is uncooperative? Maybe, but I still like this style.)

Even if you don't really want to change anything about your dog's tags, think about how clinking tags might disrupt mealtime. I've had clients perplexed about why their dog was finicky about her food at home but happily wolfed down the exact same meal at the pet-sitter's house. A little investigation revealed that a low plastic plate rather than a high steel bowl reduced the noise that was interfering with the dog's ability to eat in peace! Now that she's got a new dish at home that her tags don't clank against, that pup is eating normally.

Ill-Fitting, 24/7 Harnesses

The harness industry keeps expanding. As a result, some first-time owners are given the impression that it's impossible to walk a dog even out to the car without one. I agree that they can be a helpful tool — a front-clip harness can work wonders with a dog that pulls on leash — but they must fit perfectly, and in most cases they should not be left on 24/7.

While it's easy to get a collar to fit well, a harness is another thing entirely. There are so many contact points where, depending on how the dog is sitting, moving, or lying down, the harness can cause rubbing, pinching, and discomfort. When you get a harness, it's critical to invest the time in figuring out exactly how it's supposed to fit. There is likely a video on YouTube from the manufacturer, and that's worth watching. After that, make sure you check and adjust the fit regularly, particularly if you have a growing puppy.

Even if you have a perfectly fitting harness, though, remember that in most cases it is intended specifically for leash walks. Yes, I realize that it feels like you need a PhD to get your dog into some of these contraptions, which is a big reason people simply leave them on. But gosh, would you want to wear something like that every minute of your life? Again, it's something many dogs tolerate, but why do we ask them to do that if we love them so much?

Skin, Coat, and Ear Issues

We've all had that moment when we see something on our dog that we should have found earlier: a tick, an infected ear, a mystery cut, a burr tangled deep in fur. No matter what it is, the sooner it's found, the easier it is to fix. That timing can mean the difference between an at-home treatment and an expensive vet bill — not to mention the amount of discomfort your dog has to endure.

When your life is busy and your dog is active, though, it's easy to miss these things. The more you do your own dog grooming, the more you have a chance to catch all sorts of new things: lumps and bumps, changes in fur texture, hair loss, parasites, or mats of fur that could be painful. Whether you take the dog to a groomer or not, a weekly home exam is a great idea. I now keep my tools (brush, nail clippers, little scissors, ear cleaner) in a basket near the TV, so that when we're relaxed at night I can slip over and make sure all the dogs are in good shape. If I had to walk over to the next room and get it, I wouldn't, because I'm lazy! This way, it has become a habit, and I feel confident nobody's suffering in silence.

Neglected Teeth

If your dog's breath is stinky and his gums are red, please schedule a dental exam with a vet. Dental problems not only cause daily discomfort but also can have serious long-term health effects, like endocarditis from a chronic bacterial infection caused by the buildup of dental calculus.

I'm all for indulging in high-end luxuries for our dogs, but I think if you asked the dogs, they'd tell you to address these five issues first.

37

MEDICAL CARE

Get the Most out of Vet Visits

Veterinary care sure is expensive, isn't it? And it's even more so when we sabotage our own pet's care. Think that sounds crazy? You figure nobody would undermine the very approach they'd just paid top dollar for?

Well...

- Have you ever been told to give your dog crate rest, but then you gave in and let her out because she barked all the time?

- Did you ever tell the vet there have been absolutely zero changes to your dog's diet — but forgot that the new Bark Box came on Tuesday filled with new treats the dog gobbled up?

- Did you ever decide not to use that ointment the vet gave you because your dog kept licking it off?

- Did you ever cut the number of ear cleanings in half because your dog hated it so much?

In thirty years of dog ownership, I have done all of these things! Now I know better.

Owners often spend considerable time researching vets to be sure they're doing right by their dogs. It's a shame when we fail to recognize that the success of that veterinary care is sometimes in our own hands. Even the best vet in the world can't help a dog whose owner didn't give the vet the full picture, didn't quite understand the vet's instructions, or didn't follow the treatment plan.

On the bright side, being a prepared, attentive, and conscientious client can help you get better value out of any vet trip.

First, Get Your Story Straight

There is a lot of hemming and hawing at the vet. "Um, let's see, maybe it was last Thursday when I first felt that lump, because I remember Aunt Sally was visiting…no, wait, that was the kitty's lump." That uncertainty paves a more tangled — and expensive — path to diagnosis.

Before you head to the vet, take out a pen and a pad of paper. Ask yourself all the questions you know the vet is going to ask you.

What's wrong? When exactly did it start? (If you waited longer than you should have before deciding to see the vet, do yourself and your pet a favor and be truthful about it.) Has it ever happened before? Could the dog have gotten into something toxic? Has the condition gotten better or worse? Have there been any other changes in the dog's health or behavior? How's behavior otherwise? Is there anything new in your routine? Have you been traveling? Has the dog had any new foods (not just the main diet but any treats or foods given to the dog by family members)? Are any other pets at home showing similar signs? If you're going to see an emergency vet who's not familiar with your dog's history, write down the exact name of any current medications.

In the heat of the moment, when pressed for answers, it's easy to forget things. That's okay. By asking yourself these questions before the appointment and writing the answers down, you can give the vet a clear, concise picture of what's happening.

Listen to that Expensive Advice

Once you've described your dog's problem to the vet, it's time for you to stop talking and listen — hard. A lot of trouble arises because people find they get home from the vet and wonder, "Wait, what did she say?" Then they guess.

Sometimes your head is spinning with worry at the vet, so it's hard to take in information. Still, you typically have three shots at it. The first is when the vet talks to you; the second is when the discharge nurse goes over the instructions; and the third is when you look over the paperwork. Even so, people often space out during all three of those opportunities to absorb the advice they are paying so handsomely for.

Try your best not to do that. Even if you are stressed out about your dog, this is the time to focus and even take notes.

Speak Up If There's a Problem

As you listen to the vet present the treatment plan, your reaction may be:

- "I don't really understand what she just said."

- "We totally can't afford that." (*Please* get pet insurance!)

- "That's not going to work, because at our house…"

No matter what the issue is, please just speak up, right there at the appointment. The vet can't read your mind, and every client family is different. It's fine to ask if you can loop in another family member to the appointment via Facetime. Sometimes the person who brought the dog to the vet forgets to mention or isn't aware of some detail that is critical.

If it takes a while for your questions or concerns to bubble up, that's fine. Call back later. Your vet will much prefer having that conversation than having her treatment plan misunderstood, to the detriment of the dog. (Your vet will likely not be available when you call, so be prepared to leave a detailed message so she can call you back with an answer.)

I'm in a bunch of dog Facebook groups, and I can report to you that it is a very common thing to post something like this: "I went to the vet, and they suggested treatment plan X. That seems wrong to me. What do you all think?" A cascade of advice follows from strangers on the internet, often contradicting the plan given by an actual medical doctor who's examined the pet and taken a detailed history. That's a disaster.

Do Not Improvise

The vet does not give you extra instructions just for the fun of it. If he says to give the meds on a full stomach, don't decide it's fine to do it earlier because it's more convenient. Yes, that steroid dosage chart sure is complicated — three pills, then two, then one, then every other day — but don't simply decide that nobody could keep up with that and come up with your own easier schedule. And don't be me, fifteen years ago, making your dog's minor fracture take four months to heal instead of six weeks because it seemed impossible to keep her from playing with the rest of the pack.

I know this stuff is hard, and you don't have time for all this extra, unpleasant dog care. Plus the dog hates it all. Skipping it is tempting, I know.

But instructions matter. These details may not seem important, but remember, you and I don't know enough to know why they are important. The vet does, and that's why we pay her. If you don't follow her advice, you might as well have skipped the appointment.

Don't waste your money. Be a great client.

THE IMPORTANCE OF AGENCY

How to Answer "May I Pet Your Dog?"

It used to be that if folks wanted to pet your dog, they just reached out and did it. Happily, in today's better-informed world, there's usually a quick, "May I pet your dog?" first. All too often, though, the response is a simple "Sure!," immediately followed by a stranger looming over the dog and swiftly sending a fist an inch from the dog's nose "to sniff." The dog — perhaps pushed forward a bit by the owner, who sees how eagerly the other human wants this inter-action — might find an enthusiastic two-handed ear jostle is next.

For some dogs — Golden Retrievers, anyone? — this moment is what they've been waiting for all morning. That extra human at-tention is the highlight of the walk. If your family has only had canine ambassadors like this, the idea that a dog might not welcome an outstretched hand is incomprehensible.

Yet, comprehend we must. Because, believe it or not, most dogs don't automatically like the whole trapped-on-a-leash-being-touched-by-a-stranger thing. As hard as it is for us to accept, that quiet dog we insist on petting may well be hating every minute of it.

Please Don't Assume Dogs Want to Be Petted

Indeed, plenty of wonderful dogs are not eager to say hello to strang-ers. They may feel anything from uninterested to wary to terrified. In some cases, they have been specially bred — by humans — to feel what they're feeling.

Unfortunately, because we humans value petting dogs so much, we ignore that pesky truth. We tend to believe that all good dogs should happily accept petting from anybody at any time. That's an odd assumption if you stop to think about it. Dogs have plenty of reasons for choosing to say no:

- Perhaps they've been bred or taught to guard, so this forced interaction with strangers is deeply conflicting.

- Perhaps they're simply more introverted and don't enjoy this kind of socialization.

- Perhaps something in their background has made them less trusting of people.

- Perhaps normally they'd welcome the attention, but today their ear hurts, or they're distracted by the German Shepherd staring at them from across the street.

There are many reasons, all legit, for wanting to skip this unnecessary interaction.

Don't Give Consent on Behalf of Your Dog

Once you're acutely conscious of just how deeply some dogs do not want to be randomly touched, you start to feel something's a little off with the question, "May I pet your dog?" It becomes clear that the consent is ultimately the dog's to give, not the human's. It feels wrong to decree, "Sure, absolutely, you go right ahead and put your hands all over this dog's body."

While dogs can't answer the question "May I pet you?" in English, they sure do answer with their body language. Unfortunately, most people don't have the skills to read what can be very subtle signals. The result? Many dogs are routinely subjected to handling that makes them uncomfortable, while they're trapped on a leash with their owner allowing it. That experience can make dogs even less enamored of strangers and — the saddest part — less trusting of their owners, who did not step up to help them through that moment.

Tips for Making Friends with a New Dog

I give my dogs agency when it comes to who touches them, and when. If somebody asks, "May I pet your dog?," I smile at their interest, and tell them I'd love for them to ask the dog. Then I show them how:

- Keep a little distance at first.

- Turn a bit to the side, so you don't appear confrontational.

- Use your warm, friendly voice to continually reassure.

- Crouch down, so that you're not looming in a scary way.

- Keep your glances soft and light, instead of giving a steady stare.

- Let the dog sniff you. But instead of shoving a fist unavoidably in the dog's face, just hang out so she has a choice of whether to come closer to investigate. Look elsewhere as she does so, so she can have a little privacy as she sniffs.

So very often this approach gets us to a waggy "Yes" from even a shy dog in thirty seconds.

How to Tell If the Dog Is Giving Consent

If the dog pulls toward the stranger with a loose, relaxed, or wiggly body, the dog is saying yes. Great! The next step is to begin petting in the spot the dog is offering — likely the chest or the rump. (A top-of-the-head pat is on most dogs' list of "Top 10 Things I Hate about Humans.")

When the dog does not give a quick "Yes," I may try backing us up a bit and making conversation, because many dogs warm up after having a few minutes at a safe distance to size up a human. When a dog is wary, I don't give strangers treats to offer, because that's going to feel stressful for the dog: "Ugh, I really want that treat, but I'm scared of that person." But I myself hand treats to the pup while the stranger is hanging out. If the dog eventually relaxes and walks over to greet the stranger, great.

If not, we simply call it a day and move along. That is also — and this is critically important — great. No harm, no foul. No need to apologize. We cheerily head on our way.

A FINAL THOUGHT

Let Go of the Vision So You Can Meet Your Actual Dog

Some of the happiest dog people I know never even meant to get a dog. Their stories run the gamut — from a stray that showed up on a vacation to a pup inherited from the too-spontaneous college kid — but they all have one key thing in common: the lack of expectations.

In contrast, one of the sadder things I see is the much-anticipated pup — long planned for, much researched — who is a continual source of frustration. From the descriptions I hear beforehand, I expect to encounter a very challenging dog. Instead, in every single case, I meet a regular doggy.

Oh, how I hate the extra burden of expectation these dogs carry. The biggest favor you can do your dog is to lose the vision and meet the unique spirit in front of you.

The Ghost Dog

The most common version of the Expectation Trap is the ghost dog. This is the looming memory of a dog who has passed on, either recently or decades ago. I hear about how these dogs were "perfect" and never [insert undesired behavior here]. The thing is, this assertion usually breaks down under a gentle query or two:

- "Gosh, he was immediately potty trained?" Well, it turns out they got him as an adult, not a puppy.

- "Wow, you never had to replace anything he chewed?" Well, it turns out that this owner was ten at the time, and her mom was the one noticing and replacing damaged items.

- "She was never jumpy and always just lay at your feet?" Well, that was absolutely true after the dog turned eleven.

Generally, we retain and savor the sweetest memories of our dear departed dogs. We remember them at their very finest hour. That's mostly a lovely thing, but it sure can be damaging to the dogs who come next.

Do yourself and your new pup a favor: try to avoid comparisons. If you can't, be sure to take off the rose-colored glasses first. They are blocking you from seeing the fresh new possibilities in front of you.

The Fictional Dog

Sometimes it's not a departed dog but a fictional one that gets in the way. Some folks have richly imagined visions of their future life with a dog, and when the reality doesn't — and can't — match up, it becomes a giant problem. Here are some typical ways the real live dog comes up short:

- **The non-dog-park dog.** That local dog park sometimes looks so fun from the outside that folks end up considering getting a dog just to be a part of it. They love to think about trotting their happy dog to his favorite place (where, coincidentally, the owner will get to enjoy that easy human socializing). When it turns out their actual dog does not like the dog park, even a little bit, the sense of dismay — even betrayal — is overwhelming. "But this is why I got a dog!"

- **The non-snuggler.** At the root of many a dog acquisition is the dream of never again watching Netflix alone. Would-be dog owners picture a nightly snugglefest on the couch. How bitter the realization, then, when the new dog turns out to be more of a dog-park dog than a hang-and-chill dog, or she prefers the nice cool floor tiles to the couch. To add insult to injury, she gets up to move if you go over to cuddle her. "But I got a dog to have somebody to snuggle with!"

- **The dog who loves the wrong person.** Sometimes a household decides that one member "needs" to have a special friend. Maybe one dog already loves the husband, so the wife needs "her" dog. Or maybe a son really wants his "own" dog. This vision delights everyone involved, so they pick a dog. Three weeks later, that dog is glued to the side of…the wrong person.

Cue the call to the trainer to "fix" things and make the doggy fit into their life just like the vision.

Lose the Vision

With most versions of the Expectation Trap, trainers can help a bit around the edges. If you get to us early enough, we can help you stack the deck. For example:

- To help create a dog-park dog, we'd be carefully exposing the pup to all sorts of safe and fun doggy friends, helping her to have a great time and build her social skills. We'd gradually move from one-on-one play to neighborhood group play, and then to the dog park when it's empty. We'd be watching like a hawk to make sure we quit while we were ahead and kept our distance from any scary trouble.

- To help create a snuggler, we'd make sure the humans learn to cherish the dog's head resting on their lap, without immediately moving in for the whole-body hug and massage. Giving the dog agency over petting is key if you have a tentative snuggler.

- To guide the dog toward loving the one he's "assigned" to love, that human has to be the source of most of the good things at first: food, play, walks. (Honestly, I'm not a big fan of this whole selected-human scenario, because I want dogs to have all the love the world might have in store for them, but sometimes there are good reasons to encourage a bond with a particular human.)

You get my drift. There are always a few things we trainers can do.

Love the One You've Got

But... There are no guarantees. My real goal in those training sessions is to get the owners to delight in the dog in front of them and to be open to the idea that this dog — this *exact* dog, without the changes they want to impose — may open up an unexpected world. Rather than working really hard, often against nature, to shove a new dog into a preexisting vision, I encourage people to be open to the experience this real live dog is just waiting there to give.

Yeah, he's terrified at the dog park. Maybe that means the two of you will take amazing hikes instead. Maybe you'll get more nature and more bonding.

Bummer, she won't cuddle. Maybe she'll draw you instead to the dog park, where you'll run into your future husband. (After all, I did! True story.)

Sometimes I think about how we dog people usually have a few dogs in our lifetime. But our dogs only have us. They live their whole lives... just with us. It would be a shame to keep wishing they were somebody else, and letting that outlook block us from discovering who they really could be — and who we could be together.

RECOMMENDATIONS AND RESOURCES

Of course, I have a list of terrific dog-related things I'd love to recommend to you. However, I'm hesitant to publish that list in a book. There is an amazing amount of energy in the dog industry right now, and that means new studies, new ideas, new products, and new people are out there for us to explore every day. I'm always learning. Just as soon as I have a favorite, I discover an even better take on it.

However, there are certainly some classic go-tos that will stand the test of time, and I'll include them below. But I'll also direct you to my website (PuppyPicks.com), where I keep an updated list of all my favorite dog things. Even better, it has links, so all you have to do is click.

Note that most of these items are available either from Chewy .com or Dogwise.com, both of which are great websites.

Products

Wire pen. You'll never regret buying an easy-to-store, light, foldable black wire exercise pen (x-pen) or two for the puppy months. You can use it to create a circular pen, block doorways, or protect bookshelves filled with chewable items. I like the ones by MidWest, with a step-through door.

Wire crate. I'm a big fan of taking your time to introduce a crate in a way that it becomes a relaxing retreat for a dog. I use the sturdy wire ones from MidWest. They're foldable, so they're easy to store or to take on vacation. I choose the ones with doors on both the short and long sides so that I can change my mind about how to orient the crate in the room.

Dog gates. I couldn't live without the pressure-mounted swing-open gates I pop in and out of my kitchen and mudroom doorways depending on which puppy guests are on the premises. The Mid-West Steel Pet Gate in graphite is my current go-to choice.

Dog bed. My favorite first beds for puppies are the small, fluffy donut-style ones that seem to help a lonely pup feel snuggled in littermate fashion. The Shag Fur Donut Cuddler from Best Friends by Sheri is my top choice. As for size, there should be just enough room for the pup to squish into the middle.

Martingale collar. Often folks tighten their puppy's regular buckle collar too much because they're (correctly) afraid the pup could slip out on a walk. That may keep the pup safe, but it's really uncomfortable all day. Instead, I hope you'll use a martingale collar for walks, which has a little loop where the leash is attached that will tighten for safety. As a first collar for a fast-growing pup, I like the inexpensive, simple quick-snap buckle version by PetSafe. Later on, when your dog has stopped growing, you can invest in a higher-quality one that even has your phone number stitched in.

Six-foot leash. In general, I'm a fan of lighter, thinner, nonstiff leashes that I can maneuver easily. For puppies, I like a six-foot leash that's about half an inch wide. There are plenty of brands that fit this description.

Long line. The long line (essentially an extra-long leash) is often left off the list of must-have equipment because folks just aren't aware of how helpful it can be for both enrichment and training. I love to take a new puppy to a wide-open park on a fifteen-foot long line, allowing the dog plenty of agency to follow scents, and then dramatically rewarding their every choice to orient themselves back to me. You might want to start with an inexpensive fifteen-footer, but as you get better at working with the length and see the benefits, you may want to upgrade to a thirty-foot version of my favorite brand: Trailblazing Tails. These leads are made of BioThane, a coated polyester webbing that's waterproof and odor-proof as well as strong and lightweight — all helpful qualities in a lead that'll drag along the ground. (Note that I don't use retractable leashes for lots of reasons, one of the biggest being that even in skilled hands, there is always some leash pressure. I'm trying to teach my dogs that a normal walk has almost zero leash pressure, and if they feel that slight tug, it's a sign to stop, move toward the pressure, and look at me.)

Treat pouch. Rather than recommend a specific treat pouch, I'll just emphasize that you need to find one you really like, because you're going to use it a lot. Want one that clips around your waist? Goes over your shoulder? Fits your phone? Has a clip for holding used poop bags? We have half a dozen in rotation at our house, because several humans walk dogs, and we all have preferences. If your local dog store doesn't have much of a selection, just look online.

Snuggle Puppy. These days I try to send each of my foster puppies to their new home with a Snuggle Puppy that's been lying around absorbing the scents of the litter for a day. The reviews from new owners confirm that this stuffed dog apparently feels at least a bit like a littermate to the puppy, thanks to its heat pack and battery-powered heartbeat. It can make a big difference in a puppy's first days and weeks away from littermates.

Toppl. If I had my way, all puppies would get at least one meal a day in the form of a frozen Toppl. This fantastic food-dispensing chew toy can play a wonderful role in giving a dog a chance to act like a dog: foraging, chewing, and licking for food. I like these better for puppies than Kongs because of their wide opening — easier for pups to get every bite, and easier for humans to clean. I moisten kibble, add a touch of something more fun (canned food, peanut butter, plain yogurt, chopped carrots, cheese), and freeze them so they are a longer-lasting activity.

Squeaky, furry tug toys. To help puppies learn that they can have some mouthy fun with their humans — but only when there's a toy in between — we need to have the right toys on hand. Get a few of the flat, furry animals (typically a fox or a raccoon) that are about a foot long, feature a squeaker in the head and the tail, and have no stuffing the puppy could unstuff.

Books

The Puppy Primer by Patricia B. McConnell, PhD, and Brenda Scidmore. This short, engaging, easy-to-follow guide can be used as an at-home six-week training program and includes specifics on how exactly to teach Sit, Stand, Come, Drop It, etc.

The Other End of the Leash by Patricia B. McConnell, PhD. Want to understand dogs, humans, and why the two sometimes miscommunicate? McConnell is your guide. A brilliant ethologist who's also a gifted storyteller, she's created a gem of a book that's a delight to read. (Also check out her searchable blog of the same name.)

Meet Your Dog by Kim Brophey. Applied ethologist and behavior consultant Brophey is leading an inspiring movement in the dog training industry, encouraging humans to think "why" before "how" when they want to address behavior. This book introduces her innovative behavior model involving a dog's four L.E.G.S. (learning, environment, genetics, self), and also outlines the characteristics of the ten breed groups, helping owners understand why, say, their cute little Aussie is herding their toddler.

Positive Training for Aggressive and Reactive Dogs by Annie Phenix. Don't let the title fool you! This beautiful book is for every dog owner and is more about preventing problems than dealing with difficult issues. It is also a fantastic tour through some of the best minds working in dog training and behavior today, as author Phenix invited sixteen top experts to contribute a chapter.

Puppy Socialization by Marge Rogers and Eileen Anderson. Socializing a puppy well involves making nuanced choices as you observe your puppy's body language. This book is a wonderfully detailed guide (including links to videos) that will help you feel confident as you approach this important task.

The Power of Positive Dog Training by Pat Miller. Renowned trainer Miller was one of the first important "crossover" voices in dog training. After achieving great success in the 1990s using then-prevailing techniques based on force and compulsion, she came to believe there was a better way. Her now-classic book on positive, relationship-based training (with lots of step-by-step instruction) is all the more convincing thanks to her background on "the other side."

Doggie Language by Lili Chin. In this tiny gem of a guide, the author uses her charming illustrations to teach in one second what I struggle to describe in a paragraph!

(Still want more? Try Karen Pryor's *Don't Shoot the Dog*, Jean Donaldson's *The Culture Clash* and *Mine!*, Leslie McDevitt's *Control Unleashed*, Kathy Sdao's *Plenty in Life Is Free*, and Suzanne Clothier's *Bones Would Rain from the Sky*.)

ACKNOWLEDGMENTS

I've often wished I could have an encouraging chat with every human who's just brought a puppy into their family. This book is the next best thing, and I'm so grateful to those who played a role in making it happen, including:

My first and dearest teachers, our own dogs (Ben, Shadow, Kela, Piper, Zoe, Eli, Rocket, Nala, Mojo, Georgie, and Kreacher) plus the 200-plus foster dogs who've given me a living classroom. (I know they probably don't read acknowledgments, but it seems so wrong to exclude them.)

My awesome clients, who trust me with their puppies and their stories.

The two giants whose brilliant courses on dog training and behavior have — I know this sounds dramatic, but it's true — changed my life: Kim Brophey and Pat Miller.

The wonderful Nancy Kerns, my editor at *Whole Dog Journal*, whose expertise in both the dog world and the publishing world has been invaluable.

The podcasters I listen to so often they're my imaginary friends, whose fascinating conversations teach me more every day: Michael Shikashio, Hannah Branigan, Allie Bender and Emily Strong, Ferdie Yau, Marissa Martino, and Ryan Cartlidge.

My delightful agent, Joan Brookbank, whose warm, loyal guidance through the mysterious world of publishing is a gift.

Jason Gardner at New World Library, whose light touch as an editor allows my books to feel like *my* books.

The amazing women in my incredibly talented writing group (Elisabeth, Paige, Rosie, Susan, and Vero), who support and push me as we all pursue that "third act."

And finally, my husband, Tom, and our daughters, Grace and Claire. They're intricately, amusingly, intelligently, and enthusiastically involved in this dog path of mine, and the sharing makes every bit of it sweeter.

INDEX

ABOUT THE AUTHOR

Certified as a dog trainer (CPDT-KA) and a family dog mediator (FDM), Kathy Callahan specializes in puppies. She and her family have fostered 225 of them in the past decade, and her dog training business, PupStart, is focused on puppyhood coaching.

Kathy writes monthly on training and behavior for the industry-leading publication *Whole Dog Journal*. Her first book, *101 Rescue Puppies: One Family's Story of Fostering Dogs, Love, and Trust*, came out in 2020. Kathy's podcast, *Pick of the Litter*, covers the ideas, approaches, and techniques that truly help people and their dogs live more happily together.

Kathy lives in Alexandria, Virginia, with her husband, Tom. They're technically empty nesters since their grown daughters Grace and Claire have moved on, but the house is still filled with warmth and fun thanks to Mojo the German Shepherd/Akita, George the Great Pyrenees/German Shepherd, Kreacher the Chow/Beagle, and Mr. Bojangles, the best cat in the world. All four pets originally arrived as fosters before becoming Callahans, and they are wonderful mentors to the foster puppies who continue to come through the household from time to time.

Check out Kathy's website at PuppyPicks.com.